THE
INNER

Erik Blumenthal Dip. Psych. (born in 1914) is a practising psychotherapist and analyst. He is a lecturer at
the Alfred Adler Institute in Zürich, President of the
Swiss Society for Individual Psychology, and Director
of the International Committee for Adlerian Summer
Schools and Institutes. He has written a number of
books on child-rearing, self-education, marriage and
old age, and is married with six children and nine
grandchildren.

THE WAY TO
INNER FREEDOM

THE WAY TO
INNER FREEDOM

A Practical Guide to Personal Development

Erik Blumenthal

ONEWORLD

THE WAY TO INNER FREEDOM

Oneworld Publications Ltd
1c Standbrook House, Old Bond Street, London W1X 3TD

Originally published in German under the title
Wege sur inneren Freiheit © Rex-Verlag Luzern/Stuttgart 1981
This English edition © Oneworld Publications 1988
All rights reserved. Copyright under Berne Convention

Reprinted 1988, 1990

Translated by Nancy Benvenga

British Library Cataloguing in Publication Data
Blumenthal, Erik
The Way to Inner Freedom:
a practical guide to personal development
1. Self-realization
I. Title
158'.1   BF637.S4

ISBN 1-85168-011-X

Printed and bound in Great Britain by
Biddles Ltd, Guildford and King's Lynn

'When one is released from the prison of self, that is indeed freedom! For self is the greatest prison.'

'Abdu'l-Bahá

CONTENTS

FOREWORD

The everyday problems we encounter can cause anxiety, confusion and a feeling of hopelessness. Stress, competition and similar conditions increasingly lead to physical and emotional disorders. In this book a renowned psychologist and psychotherapist shows us how to free ourselves of these shackles, often through the use of very simple techniques.

This is a book full of wisdom and useful advice, a book which convinces by its clarity and credibility and inspires us to follow its example.

Erik Blumenthal has already succeeded in acquainting countless numbers of people with the philosophy and the practical application of Adlerian psychology. He has been enthusiastically received everywhere. I wish him the success with this book that he rightly deserves.

Rudolf Dreikurs

PREFACE

The practical, easy-to-learn techniques of personal development described in this book are based chiefly on Alfred
Adler's discoveries in Individual Psychology. I am most
deeply indebted to two of Alfred Adler's colleagues, Dr
Alexander Müller and Prof. Dr Rudolf Dreikurs, who
introduced me to the teachings of Adlerian psychology. The
latter's contribution to the dissemination and the further
development of Adlerian psychology remains unsurpassed.
His example, his thinking and his friendship have enabled
me to put its principles into practice in my personal as well
as my professional life.

The goal of personal development is freedom from our
own negative feelings, emotions and moods, from the
competitiveness and pessimism of our age, from materialism and superstition. Through it we attain the inner
freedom which brings patience, tolerance, self-confidence
and happiness. We find peace with ourselves and with
others. It is not my intention to present this theory of
personal development as if it were scientifically watertight.
The reader who encounters difficulty in accepting any of
the viewpoints offered in this book should consider its
recommendations as working hypotheses. In this way even
the sceptical reader may be helped towards successful
personal development.

This book is primarily concerned with gaining a deeper

11

understanding of ourselves and achieving personal growth; the reader will find a more detailed discussion on developing our understanding of each other in my book, *To Understand and Be Understood*.[1] Both books are practically-oriented and aim to help the reader achieve something positive within a short time. The encouragement this brings is a further aid to applying the new techniques of personal development to all areas of our life, to our relations with our family, colleagues, friends, in the community and society at large.

1

A BRIEF INTRODUCTION TO ADLERIAN PSYCHOLOGY

Alfred Adler's Individual Psychology differs from other schools of psychology in several essential points.

It considers the person as a totality, as an indivisible whole, regardless of the number of parts into which we otherwise might divide a human being. This partitioning of the person—for example the psychoanalytical division into ego, id and super-ego, or other divisions between the conscious and the unconscious or among the functions of thought, feeling, will and action—is necessary as a starting-point from which to work. Such classifications can help us understand the human individual better, but they should never be misused by allowing the various divisions to be regarded as independent forces over which the individual has no control. It is a prejudice typical of our age to assume that the individual is regulated by such forces.

Adlerian psychology regards a human being as a goal-oriented individual and considers everything the person does from the point of view of the goal. In other words, in psychological matters it is more important to think about an action in terms of the aim it is meant to achieve than in terms of its cause. Adlerian psychology, therefore, does not search primarily for the causes and reasons, but for the goals of human behaviour, and for this reason it has also been called teleo-analysis.

An individual's thoughts and ideas play a prominent role in his behaviour; they are more important than the facts at stake because a person's actions are motivated more by his thoughts and ideas than by facts. We are relatively free in the way we form our thoughts and ideas. In Adlerian psychology this so-called free creative power makes a person responsible for everything he does, rather than allowing him the many possible excuses offered by other schools of psychology.

Adlerian psychology sees the person as a social being. This is an age-old concept; Aristotle spoke of the *zoon politikon* (political animal) who can be completely understood only in the social sphere, i.e. in his natural environment. Alfred Adler speaks of the 'iron logic' of social relations.

Adlerian psychology is a *Gebrauchspsychologie* (literally 'psychology of use') in contrast to the so-called *Besitzpsychologien* ('possession psychologies') which describe men and women as beings who possess certain qualities. In the view of Adlerian psychology the important thing is not the possession of these qualities but what the individual does with them, that is, how he or she uses them. Adlerian psychology is an optimistic psychology, in that it regards optimism as a justified attitude to life and pessimism, in contrast, as unwarranted.

The social equality of all people is one of the major principles of Adlerian psychology. This means that none of the usual differences—race, sex, age, education, status, ability or other qualities—plays any part in it. Everyone, even a small child, should be regarded as an equal partner in any shared task.

Adlerian psychology represents the foundation and application of a new theory of learning; its aim is to make knowledge of human nature accessible, not through an intellectual process but through a process of transformation that reaches into the depths of the personality. It hopes to overcome the crisis of individualism and seeks to establish a synthesis between the personality and the community. The goal of Adlerian psychology is to sharpen our sense of reality, to develop responsibility and to replace hidden animosity with mutual goodwill; this, however, can be achieved only through the conscious development of social awareness and the discarding of our prejudices.

2

UNDERSTANDING
GENERAL PRINCIPLES

In order to succeed with your efforts in personal development it is essential to understand certain general principles. Some of the most important ones are discussed in this chapter. And I repeat my advice: If you find it difficult initially to accept one or more of these principles, at least try to consider them as hypotheses with which you are prepared to work.

'Unity in diversity'

'The diversity in the human family should be the cause of love and harmony, as it is in music where many different notes blend together in the making of a perfect chord. If you meet those of a different race and colour from yourself, do not mistrust them, and withdraw yourself into your shell of conventionality, but rather be glad and show them kindness.'[2]

Personal comparisons between one individual and another are inappropriate and should always be avoided because, as we shall see, they do not lead to personal development but instead are actually detrimental to it. The only acceptable reason for comparing people with one another is to obtain objective information, and for this we can only make comparisons of abilities. For instance, it is not difficult to find out which of two persons has a better command of the English language, but such information should never be used to imply that this person has more value as a human being. There are many standards of comparison that one could make which would reveal human differences, but no matter which criteria are used or what differences are brought to light, when all is said and done there is a fundamental unity which exists within the human race: in the essence of their humanity all people are 'leaves from one tree'.

The concept of unity in diversity leads us to the principle of the social equality of all people. Naturally a university professor and a rubbish collector have different abilities and qualities to offer, but this has nothing to do with their social equality. As human beings they are of equal value, regardless of how many 'talents' any particular individual may have. As has been written in the Bible, it is the use we make of our talents—the return we give on them—which is important, rather than the talents themselves.

A true understanding and application of social equality is vital if peace of every kind is to be established in the world. At present much of the human race is involved in a period of transition from an autocratic past to a democratic future. In earlier periods of history there was usually one individual who possessed ultimate authority—the king, the prince, the patriarch. (Even in our own time some fathers still try to play the paterfamilias in their own homes, although this role is becoming increasingly untenable.) Such authority figures may have been necessary in earlier times, but this sort of absolute power is unwarranted today.

Democracy is possible only when social equality and mutual respect are present. To advocate democracy, then, is not to advocate anarchy. In the family, for example, allowing children 'total freedom' would be both unwork-

17

able and undesirable (even if anyone really knew what it actually meant!). Adlerian psychology is opposed to the domineering authority of any single individual, but it is in favour of the authority of the group—whether family, community or society—and thus of the laws or rules the group makes for itself. It also upholds the authority of life, of reality, and of the highest power of all, the spiritual principle which we commonly call God.

Autocracies rule by coercion, democracies rule by persuasion. Under earlier systems everyone knuckled down to oppressive authority, but today we govern ourselves through recommendations and agreement. Nowadays we face offenders with the natural or logical consequences of their actions instead of punishing them, encouragement replaces criticism, suggestions replace orders. In the past, mistakes were denounced, today achievements are recognised. And it is not particularly important whether all of our discoveries are new; what is essential is that we put our knowledge into practice.

The danger of a certain self-conceit is often advanced as an objection to these principles. The answer to this is that obviously people are capable of misusing anything, but in applying the techniques to be discussed later they will be capable of devoting themselves to the tasks in their lives more objectively, without always hankering after success and trying to establish superiority. A person attempts to establish superiority by comparing himself with others: in other words, by moving along the vertical rather than the horizontal line.

The diagram opposite shows what we mean by this. The line from P (past) to F (future or goal) represents the course taken by the 'normal' person. The so-called normal person in this example, however, is only hypothetical; no one exactly like this really exists. In real life the normal person

18

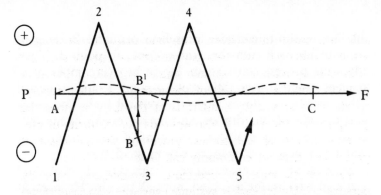

does not move through life obstinately toeing a straight line; instead, as he goes about fulfilling his life's tasks he is more likely to follow the course of the broken curved line. The space above line PF, indicated by a plus (+), represents superiority, while the space below the line, indicated by a minus (−), represents inferiority.

Now let's assume that there is a person at point 1 in the Minus Zone, someone who is not sufficiently self-confident and who feels inadequate and inferior. Of course this person is not always going to want to continue in the Minus Zone, that is, as someone inferior, instead he is going to try to achieve a feeling of superiority. How he goes about this is shown in the following diagram. For our present purposes it is sufficient to imagine that he is seeking to compensate, that is, that he wants to rise from his present state. However, in reality it is not enough for him merely to compensate, that is, to reach the 'normal' line; rather in compensating he will overcompensate, trying to rise as high in the Plus Zone as he has felt himself to be in the Minus Zone. Thus he strives to reach point 2.

If in this way or even through subterfuge he achieves a feeling of superiority, he will prefer to continue in the Plus Zone, in other words on a parallel line above line PF. But he will not succeed in this because he is accustomed to comparing himself with others, and so he will soon find

19

another reason to consider himself inadequate. Once again he will fall back into the Minus Zone, to point 3. Then the same process starts again. Again he overcompensates, reaches point 4, then falls back to point 5, and so on; in other words, he moves along the vertical line. The peaks and troughs of this line depend on the extent of his self-confidence. If, for example, his feeling of inadequacy is not acute, the peaks and troughs will be shallower.

So what are the consequences of this type of behaviour? Let's go back to the so-called 'normal' person. He starts at point A and, after a certain time in his development, arrives at point C. In other words, he moves along the horizontal line of self-development following a course represented by line AC.

Let's now consider the person with a pronounced sense of inferiority and let him begin at the same time, but at point 1. If we measure the length of line AC along the vertical from point 1 through point 2 to point 3, we reach point B. If from point B we project point B^1 onto line PF, we can see that the insecure person takes as long to travel from A to B^1 as the 'normal' person does to travel from A to C; that is, his development has been slight in relation to the 'normal' person.

Movement along the vertical line, therefore, impedes progress and hinders development. A person who travels along the egotistical, subjective vertical line instead of along the more objective horizontal line functions like a poorly-constructed engine which, instead of producing power and motion, converts most of its energy into heat through inner friction. In other words, he squanders his energy on subjective problems. He does not have sufficient power, sufficient energy at his disposal to solve life's objective problems because he has created a second problem for himself by repeatedly wanting to prove how good or how bad he is. As long as we're looking to see what kind of effect we have on others, as long as it seems important to determine or prove how good or bad we are, we'll never achieve what we are actually capable of, because we waste most of our energy in subjectivity.

Let's consider an example of this. A promising university professor had just finished a lecture which had filled her listeners with enthusiasm. Just then an old friend from her student days came up to her, congratulated her on the lecture and asked, 'How did you learn to speak in such an exciting way? Forgive me for saying so, but your lectures used to be pretty run of the mill and rather boring.' The professor replied, 'Yes, that's true. In those days a demon used to visit me after every lecture. Sometimes he patted me on the shoulder and praised me; other times he told me what I'd had to offer that day was pretty worthless. But one day I got fed up and told the demon to go to hell. My lectures have improved a lot since then.' In other words, ever since she abandoned her self-centred interest in how good or bad she was and concentrated on the objective goal of enlightening her listeners, she became a much better lecturer.

If we believe in the social equality of all people, personal comparisons between one person and another are unnecessary. Our refusal to apply the outdated autocratic scale of 'superior–inferior' enables us to jump off the current see-saw of competitiveness. We have to realise how inappropriate it is to compare ourselves with others.

Now let's consider how a person obtains a feeling of superiority over someone else through subterfuge. The diagram below helps us understand this. A compares himself with B and believes himself to be inferior. Thus he considers B to be above him. He may now try to reach B or even to surpass him. He really wants to reach point A^1, from which position he can look down on B. While A's efforts to achieve something are positive, his wish to look

21

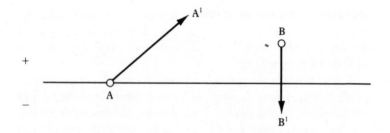

down on B must be seen as negative. If A has very strong feelings of inadequacy, he will no longer believe himself capable of achieving anything through his own efforts, so he employs the device of disparaging B in some way, by criticising him or belittling his good qualities. In this way he 'demotes' B to point B^1. He himself, however, has not achieved a thing but remains in his old position, point A, which, thanks to this trick, is now higher than B^1. In other words he has used the cheapest possible method to achieve a feeling of superiority.

No one would think of comparing an apple to a piano. And yet such a comparison would be even less meaningless than the comparison of one individual with another, because both the apple and the piano are on the material plane. To be sure, on the material plane we can measure our physical strength against that of others—in sports for example—but to compare the personal, human value of one individual with that of another is meaningless. The differences in emotional and mental qualities between one individual and another are so great that we know each individual is something absolutely unique which has never existed before and will never exist again. When we bear in mind that a person's social value derives from his mere existence and does not differ fundamentally from the social value of anyone else, we can appreciate just how meaningless such comparisons are.

Thinking in terms of levels

'What are the animals' propensities? To eat, drink, wander about and sleep. The thoughts, the minds of animals are confined to these. They are captives in the bonds of these desires. Man becomes a prisoner and slave to them when his ultimate desire is no higher than his welfare in this world of the senses.'[3]

There are many different series of levels, but for the purposes of this book we will now consider three of the levels of existence. These are the animal, the human and the spiritual levels or orders. By thinking in terms of these three levels we can better understand many things. Each level has its own laws, while at the same time being dependent on, but never regulated by, the laws of the level below. For example, a typical function on the animal level is feeling. Man, having a body, naturally shares in the animal level, even though the typical function on the human level is thinking, while on the spiritual level believing is the corresponding typical function. (Belief in this context has a wide range of meanings, not merely the connotation of religious faith. The human capacity for belief is a spiritual force whose significance is still not sufficiently recognised by science, although we already know what power this function can have.)

In another example we can see what the concept of freedom means on these three levels. On the animal level freedom does not exist, because animals are regulated by instincts and drives. On the human level we have outer freedom; however, in normal society such freedom must be limited, because a person may enjoy outer freedom only to the extent that he does not violate the freedom of a fellow human being. On the spiritual level, however—to which each individual is capable of evolving—the funda-

23

mental principle is inner freedom, and inner freedom is unlimited.

Let's use traffic to illustrate this. The driver who decided to trust his instincts alone would very quickly become a road casualty. Traffic must be regulated, and regulation means the curtailment of outer freedom so that no one, for example may suddenly decide to drive the wrong way down a one-way street. But when a person no longer sees traffic control as an imposition but instead decides of his own free will to want to do what he ought to do—that is to obey the traffic rules which exist to serve everyone—he is exercising his inner freedom.

Another example concerns sexuality. Aside from the continuation of the species, for animals sex is a matter of satisfying an appetite or drive. On the human level, on the other hand, we might describe sex in terms of mutual attraction or reciprocal happiness, while on the spiritual level sex involves total union, complete mutual surrender, true love.

Take another example. On the physical level the law of causality is all-important. We use scientific methods of counting, measuring and weighing to search out the causes and reasons for things. On the human level, however, goal orientation is of primary importance; we look not so much for causes and reasons as for goals and purposes. On the spiritual level the fundamental questions we ask concern the meaning, the sense of something.

Another example involes our means of perception. To an animal the five outer senses (which man shares) are of the utmost importance to perception. On the human level the five inner senses (imagination, thought, understanding, memory, and common sense) are more significant, while on the spiritual level intuition is the predominant instrument of perception. Incidentally, the meaning of a term may differ according to which level we are discussing. For instance animals, like people, have memory, but an animal cannot voluntarily exercise its memory, which only functions in response to certain stimuli. Human memory, on the other hand, can operate completely independently of external stimuli.

One last example. Animals are ruled by fear, while human beings, as we shall see, can free themselves from fear to a great extent. But on the spiritual level—the level of the relationship between God and the individual—however, fear of God is involved, although this type of fear has nothing whatsoever to do with being afraid. Fear of God means respecting God, loving Him, obeying Him, but not feeling afraid of Him. Thus just as authority has a different meaning under democracy as under autocracy, so fear, freedom and obedience mean different things on different levels. No doubt we can find many other examples of this principle, such as the differences between instinct on the animal level, intelligence on the human level, and, on the spiritual level, the knowledge which transcends the purely intellectual.

Another category of different levels may be found in the distinctions between the individual and the group, and here again different laws apply to each level. Individual behaviour, for example, cannot be predicted but, to some extent, group behaviour can be. In Germany some years ago, for instance, there was a surplus of between two and three million women. This meant that some two to three million women could not count on getting married. At the same time, however, not a single woman out of this group was 'condemned' to remain unmarried, for if she really wants to, every woman can find a husband, even if she has to emigrate to Canada or Australia!

The same principle applies to unemployment. In periods of unemployment, a large group of people is unable to find work, yet no individual within this group is automatically condemned to remain jobless, for a person can always manage to find some type of work, even in the bleakest times.

People shouldn't be satisfied with slogans and simple formulas. Instead we have to realise that, when we're talking about education, for example, an anti-authoritarian attitude may be appropriate on an individual level but not on a group level where, as we've seen, normal social relations are impossible without some form of external control.

All of the preceding examples are intended to stimulate thought and are consequently incomplete and chosen at random. The following diagram sets out some of our conclusions about the nature of the three orders. But it is no longer necessary at this point to continue our discussion of what we can learn from thinking in terms of levels.

Spirit	belief	inner freedom	love	meaning	intuition (inner vision)	knowledge (reasoning)	fear of God
Soul (Human)	thought	outer freedom	enjoyment (happiness)	goal	inner senses	intellect (comprehension)	fear
Body (Animal)	feeling	lack of freedom	pleasure (sex)	cause	outer senses	instincts	anxiety

The independent investigation of reality

'God has given man the eye of investigation by which he may see and recognise truth. He has endowed man with ears that he may hear the message of reality and conferred upon him the gift of reason by which he may discover things for himself. This is his endowment and equipment for the investigation of reality. Man is not intended to see through the eyes of another, hear through another's ears nor comprehend with another's brain. Each human creature has individual endowment, power and responsibility in the creative plan of God. Therefore

26

depend upon your own reason and judgement and adhere to the outcome of your own investigation, otherwise, you will be utterly submerged in the sea of ignorance and deprived of all the bounties of God.'[4]

Whatever their social status or education, modern men and women are far more capable of thinking independently and drawing logical conclusions than were people of earlier times. Two thousand years ago only a few people were capable of this, and three thousand years ago humankind was only beginning to develop this ability. In his work *The Ever-present Origin*, Jean Gebser uses examples from every field of art and science to illustrate how human consciousness has developed. Gebser's work which has had an enormous influence on the scientists and artists of our time, argues that human consciousness is in the process of evolving from the intellectual to the spiritual plane.[5]

The development of the ability to think may well bear some relation to the growth of the total extent of our knowledge. I once read that human knowledge doubled between the time of Christ's birth and 1750. Between 1750 and 1900 it doubled again, and yet again between 1900 and 1950. After that the time it took for our knowledge to double grew shorter and shorter: from 1960 to 1966 and then from 1966 to 1969. According to these calculations the total extent of human knowledge should have been doubled every three months in 1975. This development can be illustrated by the fact that 6,000 different professional medical journals were available in 1981, of which 2,000 did not exist in 1977.

What is important, however, is not speculating about the development of the human capacity to think—after all, we have invented tools such as computers which relieve us of non-creative thinking—but the need for each individual clearly to realise his own ability to think independently.

27

At present most people still have no faith in their own capacity to think and rely too much on external sources for their opinions: on their parents, relatives, friends, acquaintances and teachers, on books, the mass media and advertising. We must not simply assimilate knowledge from these sources indiscriminately, since this can lead all too easily to prejudices or to the over-reliance on science which typifies our age. Nor should we criticise everything we take in, since this leads to pessimism, indeed to nihilism and rebellion. Rather, we must subject the information with which we are constantly bombarded to critical scrutiny and accept what we recognise to be right. To do this we need a yardstick which Individual Psychology, with its concepts of social awareness and courage, provides. Another, even better, yardstick is the one provided by true faith in God.

The importance of the individual

'This challenge . . . faces no doubt primarily the individual . . . on whom, in the last resort, depends the fate of the entire community. He it is who constitutes the warp and woof on which the quality and pattern of the whole fabric must depend.'[6]

Confucius said, 'Each individual is responsible for the rise and the decline of the entire world.' Einstein put it this way: 'The person who considers his own life and that of his fellow creatures to be meaningless is not only unhappy, but almost not worthy of life.' Our last quote comes from Gebser: 'Everything, no matter how far it's destined to go, must begin with the individual and be realised by the individual.'[7]

It is true that we have too little faith in ourselves and that we're too unmindful of the importance of each individual, each person in the street, to the entire human race and its future. It is not only the politicians, industrialists and other important figures who determine the fate of the world; each individual, whether man, woman or child, whether consciously or unconsciously, is necessary to the human race and its development. The importance of the individual depends on his belief in this fact. What matters is the individual's belief in himself.

The American president Woodrow Wilson once said:

> Nations are revitalised from the bottom up, not from the top down. All that I know about history, all my experiences and observations have convinced me that the true wisdom in life develops from the individual experiences of everyday people. Life's usefulness, power and fruitfulness spread upwards from the earth like the natural growth of a great tree, ascend through the trunk to the branches and penetrate through as foliage and fruits. The dynamic power which raises the level of the individual strata of society starts with the upward-striving anonymous masses who make up the foundation everywhere. A people is only as great as its masses.

Each opinion or expectation, each display of interest or apathy, each action, belief or doubt influences other people, whether the individual is aware of this or not. We can scarcely say that anyone has even a single thought which is entirely a private affair.

Let's consider a small example. Suppose I am having a conversation with someone and a passer-by just happens to hear snatches of what I say. Perhaps some statement or another makes such an impression on her—without her even registering the source—that it completely changes her life. Neither she nor I would have realised the future significance of this accidentally overheard statement.

What we lack time and time again is faith in ourselves, and in the influence we exert, whether we want to or not.

But if we cultivate an awareness of this, our influence for the good can become increasingly important.

This anecdote, which I once found in a newspaper, can serve as an illustration. Little Peter was playing noisily in a room where his father was trying to read a book. All the father's efforts to persuade his son to play more quietly were unsuccessful, until he made one last desperate attempt. He tore out a page printed with a map of the world and ripped it into shreds. 'Here's something you can play with without making noise,' he said. 'Try to put this together again!'

Now I'll have some peace and quiet, thought the harassed father as he buried his nose in his book once more. And so he was astouned when Peter succeeded in putting the map back together perfectly in a comparatively short period of time.

'How did you do that so quickly, Peter?' he asked in amazement.

'Oh, it was easy,' said the little boy. 'See, on the other side there's a picture of a man. I put the man together, and then the world was all right too!' This gave his father something to think about for a long time.

Human goal orientation

'Let each morn be better than its eve and each morrow richer than its yesterday. Man's merit lieth in service and virtue and not in the pageantry of wealth and riches.'[8]

In the diagram opposite, the horizontal line leads from the past to the future, to a goal, a purpose, an intention. The vertical line represents the present moment: a time when things are unsettled; when we're starting a project or have something to deal with; when we're unhappy or depressed, weary or dissatisfied; when we've done something wrong;

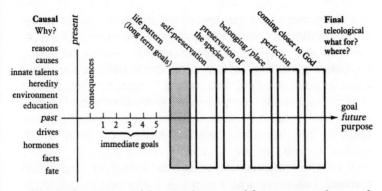

when we're angry with ourselves or with someone else, and so on.

Until recently, if we wanted to understand something, we looked backwards to the past for reasons or causes, asking 'Why?' In other words, we looked at things in terms of causality. To explain someone's behaviour, we had to take his temperament as well as hereditary factors into account. We also wanted to know about his environment, education, and so forth. And naturally we looked for extenuating circumstances: compulsions, hormonal conditions, mild brain damage or whatever. We placed too much importance on all these so-called facts.

Today, especially in the psychological context, we look forward instead of backward. We no longer ask 'Why?' but rather 'What for?' or 'Where?' This is called the teleological way of looking at things. There are a number of reasons for this complete shift of emphasis, so let's consider a few. In the first place, the factors which have led up to the actions, feelings or moods we are examining in the present belong to the past; they cannot be changed because they have already happened. Yet our future goals are always ahead of us, even if we are not aware of them. And as soon as we realise this, we can change what lies ahead, even these unconscious goals.

31

Furthermore, we can find a hundred causes for some-one's behaviour. Many psychologists are even inclined to look all the way back to the womb to find out what happened to the baby at that time. But at any given moment there is only *one* goal determining someone's behaviour. And it is easier to recognise one goal than to find causes among hundreds of factors. Besides, the force that pulls us from in front seems to be stronger than the force which pushes us from behind.

Now the question is, what goals does an individual pursue? For those who believe in a spiritual principle, in the higher power which we commonly call 'God', the ultimate goal is to come ever closer to God. The fundamental importance of such a goal is not so much that it is attained, but that it guides and inspires in the same way that the stars lead on the sailor even though he does not actually intend to reach them.

Perfection is another important goal towards which everyone strives whether or not they realise it and whether or not they even want to. In this sense perfection doesn't mean perfectionism but rather the basis for all development. An individual wants to develop towards the fulfil-ment of his own destiny using his potential and abilities in the best possible way. Take the example of a baby lying on her back in her crib, who begins to play with her fingers. This baby is pursuing perfection, because she is learning how to use her fingers and hand, although of course she is not aware of this.

Another primary goal pursued by each individual (consciously or unconsciously), is the positive goal of a sense of belonging. Every person wants to know where he belongs, what his place is. This goal motivates babies and children as well as adults. No one wants to be alone all the time because, as we know, the human individual is a social being.

On the diagram there are two further goals to the left of the goal of belonging, goals which are usually designated as 'drives'; self-preservation and survival of the species. On the merely physical or animal level we can speak of the sex drive; however, this is subordinate to the corresponding goal on the human level of the preservation of the species, that is, the reproduction of the human race. In the same way hunger and thirst, for example, are drives on the physical level which are subordinate to the goal of self-preservation.

To the left of these goals on our diagram we see life pattern, which we shall discuss later. This section is cross hatched on the diagram because, in contrast to the goals we've discussed so far, life patterns can have negative aspects. This area represents an individual's long term goals, which he is not conscious of as an adult because they spring from the fundamental attitude he formed about himself in early childhood, from his earliest assumptions about his own powers and abilities, about other people, about life and the world in general. A person's life pattern also includes the strategies he or she developed as a small child to puruse these early goals. Small children are very observant, but since they have insufficient experience and knowledge, very often interpret their experiences incorrectly, and thus may form negative life patterns as they pursue their goals.

Here are some examples of such long term goals. 'I must be good' (as we shall see, this goal is not as positive as it may at first appear). Or, 'I want to be something special,' or 'I want to be first,' or 'I want to make sure other people help me,' and so forth. Such objectives are of great significance for personal development.

The five so-called 'immediate goals' which determine our social behaviour may be even more important. We pursue one of these five goals—again, unconsciously—whenever

33

our social behaviour is out of keeping with sound human understanding or reflects a lack of concern for others; when we are dissatisfied or at odds with something; or when we are unable to live in harmony with others. These five goals are: excusing one's own faults; attracting attention; establishing superiority; retaliation; and retreat. These goals, together with an individual's life pattern, underlie one of the most important techniques of personal development.

The diagram has one further symbol, a line to the right of the present, labelled 'consequences'. We shall see later that we need only recognise the consequences of our behaviour or situation in order to identify our immediate goals.

The power of expectation or faith

' . . . the faith of no man can be conditioned by anyone except himself.'[9]

'By faith is meant, first, conscious knowledge, and second, the practice of good deeds.'[10]

To expect means to be directed towards something in the future. Expectation is probably the strongest force human beings experience in their lives. Anxiety, for example, nearly always involves expectation, that is, one anticipates that something will go wrong or be unsuccessful, for example. Obviously there are positive expectations too, which we can collectively term 'optimism'.

The optimist expects that things will go well, that he will succeed, that he will achieve something, that what he is doing has a purpose. The optimist is always justified in his optimism, because 85% of the time he does meet with success. Yet he is probably aware that his atittude contributes to his success, because, being focused on his objective, he uses his powers at the right time, in the right place, in the right way. He moves in the best possible direction; he

34

rests when it seems right to do so and proceeds when circumstances seem to advise it.

Of course, external circumstances are sometimes stronger than he is, and it may happen that he has bad luck despite his correct behaviour. This accounts for the other 15% of the time. What does he do then? First he tells himself, 'OK, I can't be successful all the time; that's life. Every day's not a holiday but why shouldn't I succeed again next time?' Then he tries to find out whether he can do things any better the next time. Full of confidence, he tackles the problem to be solved and again succeeds.

But how do things look to his opposite number, the pessimist, the human disaster area? He expects things to go wrong; he expects not to achieve anything, and belives that he is inadequate and destined to fail. He, too, is right 85% of the time. Why? Because right from the start he tackles the problem in the wrong way; he doesn't focus his energies at the right time; he moves when it would be better to rest, or rests when it would be better to move. He opens his mouth when it would be better to keep quiet, and he keeps his mouth shut when it would be better to say something. In short, he moves mainly in the wrong direction and thereby courts disaster without even realising it. But it sometimes happens that even the worst pessimist, against all expectations, meets with success. Again, this accounts for the other 15% of the time. So then what does he do? He tells himself, 'Something must have gone wrong!' But even in this case he still accomplishes what he really wants: namely, to prove that he is correct in his pessimism.

Many people regard optimism and pessimism as two opposing yet equally justified attitudes to life. Yet this is not true, because the pessimist anticipates the bad just as the optimist anticipates the good. Surely no one would say that good and bad belong on the same plane. The bad belongs in the Minus Zone, the good in the Plus Zone. Plus is superior to minus, as light is to darkness. From the individual's point of view a pessimistic attitude may seem justified, because a person can decide for himself what he wants to believe. But from the point of view of the effect pessimism cannot be justified.

Of course, by optimism we mean true optimism, not the optimism of a fool who simply sticks his head in the sand or says, 'I'll just cross the road without watching the traffic; no one will run into me.' This is not optimism, because the person who acts this way believes neither in his own powers nor in life and reality.

We often come up against the rationalisation technique called 'calculated pessimism'. But again this cannot be justified, because it is a way of avoiding disappointment, and this is a sign of weakness since it shows that a person feels unable to bear disappointments. Another rationalisation is to say that our happiness is much greater if we succeed despite our expectations. In reality, however, we are in a position, and have the power, to cope with things. As we shall see, we don't even need to make ourselves feel disappointment when we don't succeed. In any case we do not need to fool ourselves and so the trick of calculated pessimism loses its meaning.

Since the power of expectation plays such a large part in personal development, it ought to be mentioned here that we could just as easily call it the power of faith. 'Faith' in this context has a comprehensive definition as a human function which naturally includes, but is not confined to, religious faith. Recent experiments with 'placebos' indicate that this human power is receiving more attention and can no longer be scientifically denied. Placebos are dummy medications, medicines which look real but are actually not medicines at all, being made from ingredients such as water, flour, colouring and so forth, which have no healing

36

properties. A recent series of experiments with placebos has shown the following results:

Placebos were given to a relatively large group of doctors who were told to pass them on to their patients. In one large experiment carried out on thousands of patients, results indicated that two-thirds of the participants were cured by the placebos. They believed—one could also say they had faith—that it was real medicine which was helping them. Similar experiments had been carried out previously from time to time, but one of these large experiments was expanded by using a double blind.

In the second stage of the experiment placebos were again given to a fairly large group of doctors, but this time the doctors, too, were led to believe that they were real medicines. So the doctors gave these placebos to their patients in good faith, with the result that nearly 90% of the patients were cured. This astonishing result was reached because the patients' faith in the medicine was compounded by the doctors' faith and, moreover, because the patients' faith in the doctors was much greater than during the first stage of the experiment when the doctors had prescribed the placebos with a certain amount of scepticism. Naturally the patients were not aware of this scepticism, yet they sensed it nonetheless, just as in the second stage they sensed the doctors' belief that the medicine would help them. In the second stage the faith which played a role in the healing process was, so to speak, tripled.

Our knowledge about the power of faith or expectation is still incomplete, but there is no question that it exists. An understanding of the power of expectation or faith can be very useful in personal development. We can be aware of our expectations at any given moment. For example, do we believe that something will go wrong or well; that we have a chance or that we shall fail? Let's consider some more examples.

37

A beginner cyclist who still feels very unsure of himself looks for a quiet street without much traffic in order to practise. Suddenly, in the middle of the empty street, he sees a big rock right in front of him. Because he is nervous he will probably ride right over the rock even though there is plenty of room on both sides to avoid it.

There are some very extreme examples too. The story of the worker locked in a refrigerator car, which took place in the USA some time ago, is especially well-known as well as being scientifically validated. A loading worker was inadvertently locked into a refrigerator car at a railway freight depot. About twenty-four hours later, when the car was opened at another railway station, the worker lay dead in the car, his body showing symptoms of having frozen to death. It was then established that not only had someone made the unbelievable mistake of locking the man in the refrigerator car, they had also made the equally unbelievable mistake of forgetting to turn on the cooling system when they closed the door. When the car was opened the temperature inside was found to be quite normal. What had happened?

The worker must surely have tried to attract attention, but because of the noise at the depot and the thick insulation of the refrigerator car, no one heard him. Now, the man was certainly aware that the cooling system was always turned on when the car was closed. He also knew that the car would not be opened again until it reached another station twenty-four hours later, and that the human body could not tolerate its low temperatures for more than two to three hours. So he was convinced he was going to die. Due to this belief, this expectation, he died unnecessarily. Things like this don't happen every day, but it does show what a strong influence the power of expectation can have. The man's body even showed symptoms of hypothermia, although the temperature was normal!

An Indian psychologist reports that in India people frequently die after being bitten by snakes. Sometimes one of these snakes may later be discovered—in the house, for example—and found not to be poisonous at all. Many snakes in India are poisonous, however, and because Indians know this and believe they will die from a snake bite, they even die from the bites of non-poisonous snakes. A similar case involves the curses put on absent people by medicine men or magicians in Australia, the South Pacific, Africa or South America. Reports that the magician's victims die several days later are well attested.

With the power of expectation we can influence not only ourselves, but also others. Many people are familiar with the way an adult's expectations can affect children, whether the adult is a teacher, parent or other relative. One example is the story of a six-year-old boy who went to stay with his grandparents. He was the 'baby' of the family and both parents spoiled him and found it hard to deny him anything. As a result, he had become accustomed to manipulating his parents and demanding his own way all the time, he spoke in a very childish manner, and he developed very fussy eating habits which made life difficult for his mother. After a few days living with his grandparents, the boy's attitude had changed dramatically. He soon realised that his tantrums did not achieve anything, and that his childish behaviour would not win him the attention he was used to. His grandparents' expectations of good behaviour were strong enough to encourage him to change. They also had faith in him, and in his capacities. His parents were amazed at the well-mannered boy who returned, and delighted that his appetite was now healthy and normal. However, it was not long before his parents' expectations of him—their acceptance of his childish ways and lack of faith in his potential—had effected a reversal.[11]

Another well-known example concerns two men who

approach one another along a dark, empty street. Each man hears the other's steps and imagines him to be a criminal intending to attack. Both men are peaceable citizens, but as the other's footsteps approach they become more and more terrified until when they finally meet they suddenly go for each other's throats simply because each believed the other would attack first.

Our last example shows how the power of expectation can influence animals as well as ourselves or other people. Some years ago the press reported the case of a small boy who was literally torn limb from limb by a Great Dane. It happened like this. A man was taking the dog for a walk on its lead and he met the little boy. Suddenly the dog broke loose—something it had never done before—jumped on the boy and savaged him right in front of his horrified master's eyes. The boy was taken to hospital where he died of his injuries a few days later. Before he died, however, he regained consciousness long enough to declare that he had done absolutely nothing to the dog: he had only had a terrible fear of it.

In this case the dog had certainly sensed the boy's fear and its reaction was not so different from that of an adult towards whom a small child shows fear. Of course we adults believe we are harmless, and faced with this situation we tell the child he does not have to be afraid. If he persists in his 'unreasonable' fear in spite of this, in our efforts to persuade him of our harmlessness we become more and more annoyed, until we end up in such a state that the child is convinced he was right to be afraid of us in the first place.

The individual as a decision-maker

'All that which ye potentially possess can be manifested only as a result of your own volition.'[12]

Day in, day out a human being makes decisions. However, very few of these decisions are made consciously, a fact whose significance is difficult to over-emphasize. This new understanding is of great importance, but it seems to be very difficult for modern people, because we are not accustomed to the idea or have not yet realised that we make decisions not only consciously but also, mostly, unconsciously. There is no word in our language to describe this fact, so we have to distinguish between conscious and unconscious decision-making. Many people today find it extremely difficult to see or accept that we unconsciously decide even our feelings and emotions. For instance, we often say, 'This person made me angry,' because we have not yet understood that no one on earth can make us angry besides ourselves. It is *our* anger, which only we can control! But this occurs mostly, of course, on an unconscious level.

The way our unconscious decision-making powers may be used on the material level can be illustrated with a very common example. Every motorist who sees a bend, a crossroads or a hill on the road ahead automatically shifts down from fourth to third gear. This decision is made unconsciously since the driver does not say to himself, 'There's a bend up ahead, I must decide to change gears.' Simple efficiency necessitates this unconscious mechanism, for if we had to make all our decisions consciously we would never get round to doing anything.

It is even more usual to make unconscious decisions on the mental level. Thoughts and feelings, expectations and beliefs are all an individual's own. In the final analysis we are responsible for all our actions and behaviour, and even for our personalities and qualities. To accept this responsibility—that is, to give up making excuses—is not easy. We all want freedom, yet we do not want to accept the responsibility it entails, preferring instead to relinquish

41

more and more of it to the state, to institutions or to other people.

At first glance this view of the individual as a decision-maker seems to have great disadvantages, because it means we do not have many excuses left. However, the disadvantages of accepting this responsibility for ourselves are only ostensible, because responsibility brings with it the inner freedom and strength we need to cope with ourselves, with other people and with life in general. This responsibility only seems a disadvantage because we find it hard to imagine the benefits of inner freedom if we have not yet experienced it. Actually, accepting full responsibility for ourselves is a positive benefit, not only because it makes us stronger and more independent, but also because it makes us more sensitive and aware, gives us more control over our own lives, and allows us to be more useful to and exert a positive influence on others.

The new

'We have, then, called into being a new creation, as a token of Our grace unto men.'[13]

People today appear to be very receptive to new things, but in fact we are not. We applaud novelties, gadgets and technical achievements because they promise us comfort and entertainment without requiring any effort from us. But we shy away from things which are truly, fundamentally, new because we have to go through a learning process in order to understand them. 'Learning' has been forced on us from early childhood, and many people rebel against what they have been taught to think of as an onerous necessity by refusing to learn anything else once they leave school or university. Moreover, new ideas entail a process of transformation, a sort of death and rebirth in that the old must die to make way for the new. But human beings are resistant to the idea of death, and consequently we resist new ideas.

Usually the new implies some criticism of the old. Since no one likes admitting mistakes or being forced to revise ingrained habits and attitudes, we develop a vested interest in maintaining the status quo. We resist the inevitability of the old making way for the new by inventing excuses such as, 'It's all been done before.' Slogans such as this militate against progress and development, including our personal development. We are all so blinkered by the past that we find it difficult to see and respond to new ideas. W. Jensen expressed it like this: 'The person who makes a prediction is laughed at for years. When the discovery is finally understood everyone says, "Of course!" '

The familiar also offers us considerable support and security. We have built up our world, we know our way around in it, and, out of emotional and mental laziness—and a love of comfort—we feel disinclined to make any changes. We view the old and familiar as a life-raft pitching in the sea of uncertainties. No one wants to swim away from a life-raft; it is much safer and more comfortable to cling to it however leaky it may become.

In contrast changes, particularly spiritual changes, challenge our sense of security and well-being. On the physical and emotional levels pleasure and enjoyment, the so-called minor pleasures (see chart on p. 26), offer immediate and tangible gratification. Consequently we are inclined to reject the major pleasures, the spiritual, as involving too much risk and effort since we are required to follow a long and laborious path in order to obtain them. They are also less tangible. Moreover, the more we progress along the spiritual path, the more our consciousness expands, and the more we are able to perceive our possible sources of error. This exposes us to a greater risk of personal conflict and doubt. Following such a path, however, does not mean

43

that we will necessarily lose sight of our goals or deviate from the right direction. At this stage we often think that it will be difficult to find our place again, and with it our familiar sense of security and belonging. However, this is a transient phase, and represents a positive sign that we are actually moving in the right direction—towards personal growth.

Spiritual changes always require new ways of thinking and new ways of applying such ideas. Einstein put it like this: 'A new way of thinking is necessary if humanity wants to survive! That is the most pressing problem of our time.' And Henrich Heine said, 'Every age which acquires new ideas also acquires new eyes.' We have a responsibility to acknowledge and try to respond to the new. As it says in the Bible, 'Lay aside the old person with his former way of life; instead renew yourselves in spirit and look at the new person, who is created in honest righteousness and holiness in the image of God.'

'As-well-as'

'The man who makes a piece of note paper to the best of his ability, conscientiously, concentrating all his forces on perfecting it, is giving praise to God. Briefly, all effort and exertion put forth by man from the fullness of his heart is worship, if it is prompted by the highest motives and the will to do service to humanity. This is worship: to serve mankind and to minister to the needs of the people.'[14]

Until recently we tended to think in terms of 'either-or'. We wanted a one-sided, single-track view of the world; we wanted to be able to file everything in its own little pigeon-hole, and hoped that this would keep things tidy and comfortable. The fact is that generalisations stem from our insecurity. We look for guidelines, for dogmas and yearn for the absolute which, in the final analysis, however, always remains outside our grasp. For instance, there is no 'most beautiful woman in the world' or 'strongest man on earth'. We can always imagine somebody stronger or more beautiful. There is only one absolute—God—and Him we cannot imagine at all.

Today we realise that the 'either-or' point of view is obsolete and reductive, and recognise that the new 'as-well-as' principle is both necessary and progressive. Everything in the world has at least two sides, and more than one explanation. Modern physics demonstrates this beautifully by defining light as two things, both wave and particle, the one definition as valid as the other. Under our old habits of mind, we would have defined light as either the one thing or the other. Today we know that it is both wave and particle, even if both cannot be observed simultaneously.

Let's take an example from the field of psychology. It used to be held that freedom could only exist without order, or order without freedom. But neither is true, for freedom without order leads to anarchy, while order without freedom leads to violence and oppression. The only true possibility is freedom *as well as* order, when freedom means the ability to act independently as long as one does not violate the freedom of others, and order serves collective rather than sectarian or individual interests.

The 'as-well-as' principle is imperative in child-rearing as well as in personal development. A child can not only be either industrious or lazy, he can also be both. He may be lazy, for example, when schoolwork or household chores are involved. But he may be industrious in pursuing his own interests in his leisure time, with his stamp album, for example, or when he is building himself a treehouse.

3

RECOGNISING
COMMON PREJUDICES

'Man must cut himself free from all prejudice and from the result of his own imagination, so that he may be able to search for truth unhindered.'[15]

Prejudices undermine unity and order and generate defeatism. To be prejudiced is to be ignorant. There are two main types of prejudice; religious prejudice and social prejudice. Religious prejudices lead to superstition. Social prejudices fall into the various categories of racial, national, economic, gender and personal prejudices. Prejudices are based on an uncritical acceptance of the opinions of others, on imitation and on subjectivity. They crop up when a person has neither the faith nor the will to think things through for himself and represent derivative, second-hand ideas. In general prejudices have three major consequences:

1. They perpetuate ignorance.
2. They hinder development.
3. They cause psychological illness.

Psychologists and other scholars divide prejudices into considerably more categories than we use in everyday life, for example the so-called 'obligatory' prejudices which are generally positive, because they spring from love, faith, religion and elevated moral attitudes. Such 'obligatory' prejudices include an individual's faith in another person to whom he has *a priori* attributed positive qualities.

Here, however, we are using the common definition of prejudice as a negative attitude which must be overcome, especially within ourselves. This is extremely difficult because most of us believe that only other people have prejudices. Under our definition prejudices may be thought of as subjective attitudes towards ourselves and the world which result from our negative life patterns. One of our chief problems in getting rid of our own prejudices is what is called 'tendentious apperception', which means seeing things the way we want to see them (even if unconsciously). No one sees objective reality; instead each of us sees through our own subjectively tinted glasses, which distort reality. So for almost everyone reality is defined not by objective events but by subjective experiences and the opinions and prejudices we form from them. A good example of this is the contradictory testimony given by the various witnesses to a crime or accident.

One day students attending a university lecture heard an argument brewing outside the lecture hall. The argument grew louder and louder on the other side of the closed door. Suddenly the door was flung open and two men dashed in hurling abuse at each other. At the height of the tumult one of the them suddenly drew a revolver and fired a shot, whereupon both men rushed out. After the students had recovered from the initial shock some of them ran after the men but failed to find them. When everyone reassembled the lecturer asked the students to write answers to some questions concerning the incident. Collecting the written replies he admitted that he had staged the entire incident in order to find out how the witnesses would interpret it.

47

When the answers were analysed it emerged (as the lecturer had anticipated) that the students' reports contradicted one another even over the simplest questions. Opinon was even divided as to which of the two men had fired the shot, although one ought to have been able to assume that the students involved—it was a psychology class—would have learned to observe carefully either from their studies or of their own accord.

Another good example of tendentious apperception is the case of the flowering apple tree set in a beautiful spring landscape. First a painter passes by, sees the play of colours, light and shadows in the branches and leaves, and decides to do a painting of the tree. Then a poet ambles by, looks at the flowers, listens to the birds singing, and decides to write a poem. A little while later someone else comes along who notices the few dead branches and wilted leaves which survived the winter. (This, needless to say, is a pessimist.) After that a farmer looks the tree over and calculates the yield on apples he can expect this year. Then a timber merchant comes along and, noticing the tree's beautiful, strong trunk, calculates how many cubic metres of wood it might yield. Finally a lover approaches. He notices the tree's shadow and the soft grass under it and imagines how lovely it would be to lie under the tree with his beloved. Anyone asking each of these six passers-by what he had seen would never get the idea that every one of them had been looking at the same spring landscape and the same blossoming apple tree.

Let's look at one more example, since it is important to our personal development that we have a clear understanding of tendentious apperception. Two men stand chatting at a busy junction in a large city. Suddenly their conversation is interrupted by a loud crash. Two cars have collided. Police and ambulance sirens add to the din, and when the entire commotion is finally over one man says to the other. 'This crazy traffic is always causing accidents. The papers are full of stories about car accidents. People are insane!' His friend, who has been standing right next to him all along, says, 'My God, they're lucky! One of those guys can still walk, and the other doesn't seem to be too badly hurt. What amazing good luck!' Both men have been through the same experience, both alter the objective reality according to their personal point of view, their own particular pair of coloured glasses. The first was a pessimist, the second an optimist.

Now let's take a look at some of the most widespread forms of social prejudice.

Heredity and environment

'Regard man as a mine rich in gems of inestimable value.'[16]

The idea that an individual is the product of heredity and environment is a prejudice which is hard to root out. Both of these factors naturally play a very important part in the development of a person's character especially when we consider that inborn talents come under the category of heredity, and education under the category of environment. This view has led to recurrent discussions, even in scientific circles, of the relative importance of nature or nurture. People who accept the autocratic tradition tend to emphasise the importance of innate qualities while others attribute greater importance to what an individual learns and experiences. Both factors are important, but neither can influence human beings to the same extent as they do animals, for example. And both factors have the wonderful potential to excuse unsuccessful child-raising or justify individual shortcomings.

Adlerian psychologists regard a third factor as even more important than heredity or environment: an individual's free creative power. 'We are all adaptable.' This is as true of intelligence as it is of learning. A weak student has decided to be weak. Of course, in saying this I am referring to the normal student of average health, who is intelligent enough to get A-levels, without any extraordinary effort. When we learn to stop discouraging our children so much, those of average intelligence (with say an IQ of between 95 and 105) will, in the not-too-distant future, be able to acquire the knowledge of today's A-level students as early as ten years old. It goes without saying that this will require new methods of teaching and learning.

If this sounds far-fetched it is because we still have an incomplete understanding of human potential. Some time ago a survey was conducted among the best-known representatives of the different schools of psychology to find out their views on the extent to which modern men and women develop their abilities. Although the different schools disagree on many points, their agreement on this particular issue was astonishing. Most of the psychologists surveyed believed that the average person today does not fully develop more than about 15% of his or her abilities.

According to this estimate 85% of our abilities remain undeveloped. Yet we might develop as little as 10% of our true potential. This is not a pessimistic view but, on the contrary, an optimistic one, for it is based on a much richer view of human beings. It means that our intelligence and other abilities could enable us to achieve far more than we can even conceive at present. It is nice to imagine how much we can still learn and develop, what we can still look forward to. Here we ought to remember the notion of 'movement on the vertical line' and its resulting waste of energy discussed in Chapter 2.

The following illustration demonstrates how rich our potential really is. The small child makes a decision and by doing so eliminates as much as 50% of all his options. He makes another decision and another 50% of the remaining options are excluded. And he continues this process till he dies, but right to the end he still has enough options to make his decision. That is how rich the individual really is. So in contrast the view of human beings which assumes that we inherit every skill and character trait from our parents or ancestors is a truly miserable one.

Even a child is capable of forming opinions, thanks to his free creative power. As a child, a person forms his personal attitudes, based on the realities around him, and from these attitudes he develops his life pattern or, as Adler termed it, his 'style of life'. (This is discussed in detail in Chapter 5.) A child is relatively autonomous in his use of his creative power, a fact which can be observed in twins. It used to be thought that twins always experience things the same way, unlike other children who from the outset experience their upbringing in quite different ways depending on their position in the family as younger or older children. However, an unpublished study I conducted on identical twins showed that each twin also experienced his or her position in the family differently.[17] The most important thing to twins was thought to be to profit from their twin-ness, to gain special status and attention from the fact of being twins. But my findings showed that twins are not satisfied with this. Each twin wants to secure advantages from his position within the family as well. And so without exception identical twins always know which of them is older and which is younger, even if the difference is only one of minutes.

In this study I asked the parents which of their twins was older. One of the mothers answered that her children were both the same age since they'd been delivered by Caesarian section. She became annoyed when I explained that the twins knew exactly who was older, which in fact they did. All twins have reached an agreement about this

51

issue, even if unconsciously. We can no longer regard the position of twins in a family as being that of a single individual because twins themselves assume different birth ranks within the family constellation. Thus, for example, if twins are born into a family that already has one child, the older twin becomes the second child and the younger twin the youngest child. In this case the older twin becomes the middle child of the three siblings. In the chapter on the family constellation we shall see what significance this has for the development of the individual child. Suffice to say here that modern twins are just as competitive as other children.

Of the three factors—heredity, environment and creative power—Adlerian psychology considers the last to be the most important. Environment, including upbringing, ranks second and heredity comes third. People's tendency to use heredity as an excuse is something therapists see all the time from the sort of parents who come for consultation swearing from the beginning that their child's problems have been there since birth and that granny was just the same. These parents fail to understand that they are creating excuses for their own shortcomings as parents because they have insufficient faith both in themselves and in their child.

Self-preservation and survival of the species

It is commonly held that human beings are regulated by two drives: self-preservation and survival of the species. Self-preservation, it is believed, includes the so-called 'aggressive impulse', while survival of the species includes the 'sex drive'. But this view, too, must be considered a prejudice. Indeed, animals are regulated by these two drives, but we must presume that additional impulses govern human beings, who belong to a higher order. As we saw earlier, both of these human needs exemplify not so much drives as goals: the goals of remaining alive and reproducing the species.

However, there is a third need which was mentioned earlier, and which I believe to be of overriding importance: the need to feel that we belong. The social factor of being included, of knowing where we belong, is more important than preservation of self or species. We can see this in the case of suicides, who do not feel they belong anywhere and give in to despair. The suicide hopes that at least his voluntary death will win him recognition.

'Facts'

The overestimation of facts is often referred to as 'factophilia'. But facts themselves are actually less important than what we make of them. In my discussion of tendentious apperception I gave several examples to demonstrate that each person interprets a fact in a way which suits his own attitude to life. Let's consider another example of this.

A first-born child, let's suppose, remains an only child for two or three years and has his mother's love and attention all to himself. Suddenly, along comes a little brother or sister. The first-born now sees that his mother no longer has as much time for him as she used to, because she is busy with the new baby. This observation is correct, but the child's interpretation of it is a subjective one, as if he were saying to himself, 'If Mother no longer has so much time for me it means she no longer loves me so much, or she loves the new baby better.' It makes no difference here whether or how much the mother really loves her first-born: the child will still act and live according to the opinion that she prefers the new baby.

We can see from this and from the previous examples that a search for the facts often results in false conclusions.

What matters is understanding what goes on inside a person when he is considering a particular fact.

Willpower and lack of willpower

The prejudice about willpower or lack of willpower is widespread because it is so easy to use this as an excuse. If we do not succeed in some task, it is because we have not had the energy or because we lack willpower. That always sounds better than having to admit simple failure!

Whether the will, incidentally, even exists at all on the human level is a moot point, but one we do not have time to go into here. Psychology textbooks always list the four classic human functions as thinking, feeling, willing and acting. Feeling, however, probably already exists on the animal level, and today the question of whether the function of willing exists on the human level is open to doubt. In any case let's leave this question open and use the term 'decision-making' instead of 'willing'.

How often do we hear someone say 'Where there's a will, there's a way'? Of course it is ridiculous to assume that absolutely anything can be achieved with sufficient willpower, yet this proverb implies that if we fail it is beause we have not had enough willpower to do the job. But we must not take this implication seriously any longer.

Here is a familiar example. If I am offered a cigarette and reply that I am a committed non-smoker, the typical response is something like, 'Oh, you lucky man!' What the smoker really means by this is that he is, so to speak, the victim of smoking. He is convinced that he simply cannot give it up, even though he knows it would be better for his health if he did.

The prejudice lies in our assumption that each person has a certain amount of willpower, this person more, that person less. To believe that one person possesses more drives than another is 'possession psychology'. But Adlerian psychology is far more interested in what a person does with what he possesses. As long as we keep such careful tabs on the qualities we possess it is all too easy to find excuses: whatever it is we need, we haven't got enough of it.

Adlerian psychology asserts that what matters is not how much energy someone has but whether he achieves what he knows to be right for him. The instant he takes steps to do this the necessary energy materialises by itself. As long as we keep asking whether we have enough energy and willpower, we unintentionally encourage failure through this doubt. But if we do not even bother about how much willpower we have or don't have, but just do what we have to do, we are much more likely to succeed. We have already established that average intelligence is more adequate for carrying out our life tasks than is commonly believed. In the same way, our natural share of willpower is sufficient to carry out our life tasks. Of course people occasionally meet with extremely unfavourable circumstances, but this happens much less frequently than we think.

The smoker who replies, 'You lucky man' is really aiming to show he hasn't got enough willpower, because this view of things is very convenient for him. Right from the start he has a familiar excuse ready whenever he needs it. When someone has managed to stop smoking for several days, he boasts to everybody he knows about his willpower, bragging that he has not smoked for a whole fortnight. If someone behaves like this he will probably start smoking again eventually, because as time goes by he will not impress his friends so much any more and, losing faith in his own willpower, he will go back to his cigarettes.

Fritz Künkel tells the story of the man at the high diving-board of a swimming pool, who takes a run-up to the board and brakes to a halt at the last minute instead of diving in. He goes back, takes another run-up and stops again at the last minute. At last, at his third try he dives into the water. If this man really wanted to dive into the water, why didn't he do so at the first go? And if he didn't want to, why did he do so the third time round? Künkel discovered that the diver was merely testing his willpower. Once he had followed through on his third attempt he could go home proud as a peacock and brag about his self-control.

This method, then, is quite simple: you set up an obstacle for yourself, hesitate before it a couple of times, and finally overcome it thus showing how much willpower it took. If we want another example we need only think of the standard Western film in which the hero gets pushed around at first but emerges victorious in the end. If he had been a winner from the beginning it wouldn't have been nearly so exciting and convincing. We show what heroes we are by first setting up obstacles for ourselves and then tearing them down. This has two advantages: not only do we emerge as heroes but we also have an excuse ready in case we fail.

To summarise: What is important is to do what is necessary, whatever a situation objectively requires. Sufficient willpower then materialises by itself. But the minute we distract ourselves by asking whether we have got enough energy, we may very well find that we don't. This is the best reason for starting with a positive outlook at the beginning so as not to conjure up doubts and fears about whether we can cope.

Failure mentality

'Heed not your weaknesses and frailty; fix your gaze upon the invincible power of the Lord.'[18]

In modern society we tend to use mistakes as a starting

point; it is a widely held belief that we learn best from mistakes.

Here is a little example of this from the perspective of Adlerian psychology. Suppose a boy makes twelve spelling mistakes in a dictation test; the teacher not only underlines the mistakes but also writes '−12' and the mark in big letters at the bottom of the page. The unconscious effect on the pupil is to make him say to himself. 'Twelve mistakes in this little test—I'll never learn how to spell!' He is discouraged by his mistakes.

An Adlerian psychologist would approach this differently. She would mark the mistakes but, assuming the dictation had 100 words, she would write '88 correct' at the bottom of the page. In this case something different happens to the child. He says to himself, 'Eighty-eight words correct out of a hundred—that's a high percentage, that isn't bad.' And so instead of being discouraged, he asks himself, 'Why can't I get eighty-nine or ninety right next time?' How often do we assume we are acting from a sound understanding of human nature when we use mistakes as a starting point, and fail to notice how much we discourage one another by this failure mentality?

We cannot build upon mistakes, upon the negative. If we make mistakes ourselves we should not treat ourselves the way a bad teacher treats his pupils, but should realise that 'To err is human'. Of course we make mistakes, but they won't get better by our dwelling on them. Naturally we have to recognise we have made a mistake, but that is the end of the matter; it is relegated to the past. The mistake no longer concerns us; instead we know we will do things a bit better next time. Whatever is involved, we should never build upon mistakes, either in ourselves or in others.

Wanting to be good

'As soon as one feels a little better than, a little superior to, the rest, he is in a dangerous positon'.[19]

This prejudice is closely connected with the previous one. 'Wanting to be good' as a long term goal is not altogether a positive one. We are usually not satisfied with simply being good for its own sake; we really want to be better than someone else. In this way it becomes negative. We compare ourselves with someone else, find something that isn't as it should be, and try to outdo the other person. This kind of 'wanting to be good', which is so often considered positive, actually achieves the opposite of what we intend. To reiterate a point made earlier: only when we are no longer obsessed by how good or bad we are can we really become better.

When someone flexes his muscles to impress people he is wasting his energy since he is not achieving anything positive, such as doing work. But he himself feels the exertion because he has allowed opposing groups of muscles to fight each other as it were. The inner struggle, the struggle with oneself, becomes even clearer if we think of a stutterer who summons up all his conscious willpower to bring out a word, but fights against it with his unconscious 'will'.

Take another example. Someone cannot fall asleep but he struggles with himself trying to. One could say that the conscious will is wrestling with the unconscious will which does not want to go to sleep for some reason, usually to achieve some goal. This kind of inner struggle usually results in failure, in wasted energy. The person involved is like a motorist who presses the brake and the accelerator simultaneously. We avoid these mistakes in the machines we invent, but commit them in our dealings with ourselves

58

when we worry about how good or how bad we are, that is, when we 'want to be good'.

As long as it is important to us to be good we act self-centredly, which cannot be right. But if we tell ourselves that whatever happens we will do our best regardless of the outcome, if we have this self-confidence, this faith in ourselves, we really can achieve better results than when we make great efforts but in the wrong direction.

Let's look more closely at the example of the insomniac because insomnia is one of the commonest neurotic attitudes. Our difficulties in falling asleep begin when we say to ourselves, 'Look, it's very late, you've been awake long enough. You've got to fall asleep now because tomorrow you have to do such and such and you must be well rested.' At this point the battle, so to speak between the inner, unconscious will and the outer, rational will begins. The outcome depends on which 'will' is stronger.

Another common example is anger. We don't want to get angry. So the next time we do get angry we begin to get angry about our anger itself. This only makes things worse. As we shall see, the important thing is to acknowledge our motive for anger or insomnia. When the motive is recognised the anger or sleeplessness will go away by itself.

It is not so easy to admit that 'wanting to be good' is a bad goal because living in a Christian society we have been taught to love our neighbour, which means being good. This is fair enough, but the important thing here is not to set up 'being good' as a goal for oneself, but to achieve it anyway. Christ gave us the essentials in the Sermon on the Mount some 2,000 years ago. But how many of us can say we live according to these teachings? Unfortunately the techniques we have developed for being good have not so far been very successful.

Therefore it is advisable to accept ourselves as we are.

We must start from the standpoint that at present we are good enough and do what we can. Whether this is really true is not that important for the moment because when we direct our energy objectively towards achieving a goal instead of struggling with ourselves, we do become better and more loving. We have to start from what we actually can achieve in order to come closer—however small our steps—to our goal.

That we actually prevent ourselves—through our own inner struggle—from succeeding can be demonstrated by the so-called 'paradoxical intention'. A stutterer comes for treatment admitting he always stutters in front of his superiors. He is told that at these times he is battling with himself and that the next time he is with one of his superiors he must try to stutter even more than usual, more than he has ever stuttered before. When the time comes he usually cannot do it. He is so used to struggling with himself that when he actually orders himself to stutter he cannot manage it. This, incidentally, is not a speech therapy technique, but it is a good way of showing someone how he brings on or prevents such symptoms himself.

The same is true with falling asleep. If we tell ourselves it isn't really that important whether we fall asleep or not, that actually it is quite nice not to sleep sometimes because we can think about things we otherwise would not have time for, we will suddenly be 'out like a light'.

The important thing is overcoming. Overcoming does not mean compensating or over-compensating; it does not mean self-mastery or controlling one's feelings. We overcome our inclinations the instant we accept the thing that disturbs us, no longer pay attention to it, but do what the situation objectively requires. Whether we fall asleep immediately or not, whether we smoke or not, whatever it may be, it is never so important that we have to struggle with ourselves. If we take this stance we can overcome external situations as well as our own inclinations.

Neither quarrel nor give in

'Of all men the most negligent is he that disputeth idly and seeketh to advance himself over his brother.'[20]

A quarrel develops when someone wants to assert his rights. But since we cannot quarrel alone, at least one other person must be involved. Every kind of conflict is senseless, however, because conflict never achieves anything but more conflict. This makes our methods of avoiding conflict with children so important in child-rearing. Even quarrelling with ourselves is inappropriate but most people know of no options besides quarrelling or giving in.

Giving in, however, is also wrong. If we quarrel with someone we insult his dignity; if we give in we insult our own. But there is a third choice, that of trying to understand the other person. Suppose I am quarrelling with my wife, and she makes a statement which I definitely know to be false. My usual reaction is to want to assert that I am right and to prove to her that she is wrong. But it would be better for me to tell myself that while my wife's opinion is indeed wrong, there must be some grain of truth in it. After all, I've known her for a long time and I know she's not stupid. I should try to ferret out this grain of truth. So I should not contradict her right away, but instead try to understand what she means. If I make the effort to understand her, she will notice this and be more likely herself to want to understand me in return.

The moment we aim for mutual understanding we find ourselves on a higher level, achieving some degree of agreement. This does not mean that my wife and I necessarily have the same opinion, but that I tolerate and accept her opinion as she does mine. As two different individuals we are entitled to different opinions. The main thing is that we agree in our mutual love and respect. In other words we do not need to quarrel.

The aggressive impulse is often spoken of as being part of human nature. We do not automatically need to agree with this, however, because it is only one point of view. The existence of drives in the emotional sphere could as easily be rejected completely. Of course drives exist, but they are connected with our physical nature. A human being is not only a physical being, but also an emotional and intellectual being. This means that higher things than drives exist. On the higher levels drives as such are no longer found; instead the individual himself determines whether or not he will allow them to remain goals that influence him.

This view contradicts the findings of behavioural psychology. This is not to advocate the rejection of behavioural psychology, but we need not agree with it when it oversteps its bounds, that is, when it implies that something true on the animal level is also true on the human level. As we saw in Chapter 2, new laws apply on the human level. Of course, our bodies make us dependent on the animal level, but we do not need to be controlled by its laws. Our minds and our souls make us more flexible than that. Naturally, since each of us is a unity we receive physical as well as emotional and spiritual stimuli. Human beings are the only living creatures who can move from one order to another, both from above and below. A man who drinks himself senseless renounces his typically human abilities such as thinking. The same is true of taking drugs. Instead of living on the clear, conscious level of thought the person who resorts to these things descends to the animal level and renounces his or her consciousness.

An individual can live on different levels. She can choose to operate chiefly on the spiritual plane and regard the material level as something secondary. Thinking in terms of levels does not contradict the concept of wholeness. But we cannot simply conclude that what we observe of animals is also true of human beings. On the human and spiritual levels something new comes into play. For a more detailed discussion of this subject see my guide to successful relationships.[21]

Equating the doer with the deed

'Love manifests its reality in deeds, not only in words.'[22]

When someone does something wrong obviously we cannot condone it; we must disapprove of it. However, we must accept and love the doer, our fellow human being, our fellow creature, our brother or sister, just as much as we did before the misdeed occurred. Only when we have learned to distinguish between the person himself and his bad behaviour—that is, not to equate the doer with the deed—can we practise true love of our neighbour, loving the person regardless of what he or she has done.

Unfortunately equating the doer with the deed features prominently in modern child-rearing. Our reproaches and criticism make children feel that we disapprove of them as people, which is terribly discouraging for a child. Of course we must censure a child's bad behaviour, but not in a way that makes the child herself feel rejected. When we decide to love our fellow human being her misdeeds cannot prevent us from doing so.

The goal or motivation impelling us to love our neighbour is a religious one. The love of one's neighbour is taught not only by Christianity but by every other major religion as well, whether Judaism, Buddhism, Hinduism, Islam, the Bahá'í Faith or others. For someone who no longer believes in God, the social awareness and concern

63

for others fostered by Adlerian psychology can be a substitute. This will be examined in the next chapter.

Distinguishing between word and deed

'The wrong in the world continues to exist just because people talk only of their ideals, and do not strive to put them into practice. If actions took the place of words, the world's misery would very soon be changed into comfort.'[23]

Agreement between word and deed is generally the exception rather than the rule. We could even say that injustice exists in the world solely because people only talk about ideals instead of transforming them into deeds. As Chesterton remarked, 'The idea that does not try to become word is a bad idea, and the word that does not seek to become deed is a bad word.'

Distinguishing between words and deeds often entails applying a double standard. For instance, we judge other people by their deeds, actions and behaviour, but we judge ourselves by our feelings, thoughts and attitudes. This double standard makes it easy for us to deceive ourselves into thinking that we are better than other people, or at least not so bad after all.

Double standards are even applied to men and women in an attempt to demonstrate women's inferiority which, although patently untrue, is still widely accepted as fact. All that is necessary to keep this prejudice alive is to label certain qualities or abilities either 'typically masculine' or 'typically feminine'.

Different standards for adults on the one hand and children and young people on the other are common too. Admittedly adults are superior to younger people in terms of physical development, abilities, knowledge and experience, but we almost never hear about the areas in which children are clearly superior to adults. Whereas adults have learned to play roles and wear masks, children are much more open, have not yet learned to conceal their feelings and hardly ever rationalise. Because of this children are much better than adults at expressing their views and attitudes. They form personal relationships easily and have a wonderful feeling for genuineness and sincerity. Children are superb observers and discoverers and have far richer imaginations than adults, which is why they are so creative and adventurous. This example, incidentally, illustrates once again how meaningless it is to compare people with one another.

Or let's take the example of racial differences. As we all know, Germany experienced the will-to-superiority of the so-called 'Aryan' race before and during the last World War. And indeed, there is hardly a country in the world where racial prejudice does not exist. For example, in Japan there used to be a small group of people who believed the Japanese were the master race. They interpreted the fact that Japanese people have so little body hair as proof that they had evolved further than other races from their remote ancestors, the apes. People can fool themselves in any number of ways as long as it serves their own advantage. Nothing is too stupid as long as it helps someone to achieve a feeling of superiority.

How can we match our words to our deeds? Alexander Müller once said that the chief symptom of how immature and insecure we are is that we offer words instead of actions. Words excuse all our shortcomings, our unrealised potential, our reluctance really to make an effort.

This is an appropriate point to bring up the subject of dualism, a very common prejudice today. Dualism means two-sidedness, opposition, the existence of two principles which do not derive from one another, such as unity and multiplicity, spirit and matter, good and evil, body and soul. Religion usually presupposes two forces, such as God and the devil, heaven and hell, light and darkness, masculine and feminine. The prejudice of dualism—the presumption of two fundamentally opposed forces—lies at the root of all our conflicts.

The familiar saying from the New Testament, 'The spirit is willing but the flesh is weak,' is often quoted when someone wants to excuse his or her own weakness. What it actually means, however, is that the spirit is stronger than the flesh. As long as we regard feeling and understanding, rationality and irrationality, super-ego and id, right and wrong, success and failure, 'should' and 'may' as pairs of opposites, we cannot achieve inner peace, for in thinking like this we are subscribing to the superstitition, 'Two souls, alas! dwell in my breast,' and we believe in a bad ego. We feel guilty when we have done wrong, and proud when we have done right.

We ought to recognise, however, that these dualistic concepts belong to the past. In actual fact the individual is an indivisible entity possessing the integrity and potential to do what is necessary. We can use our left hand just as we do our right, our faith just as we do our understanding and feeling, and all of these are only different aspects of one and the same human being, not opposites at all. So today we no longer speak of dualism, but rather of plurality.

The unity of word and deed is indispensable to our development if we wish to have greater integrity and become more truthful, more credible. It may not be a very popular requirement, but we have to change if we wish to achieve this. We must apply the principles explained so far to our own inner lives without worrying whether we have enough energy or whether it is worth it. Agreement between word and deed can only be achieved when we have not only words but also actions to offer.

Materialism, intellectualism, need for admiration, egotism

'The master-key to self-mastery is self-forgetfulness.[24]

This is a whole group of prejudices which are very important, especially at present. We use them to distinguish ourselves from other people. In earlier times noble birth made someone a better, more valuable person than other people. Today lineage is considered less important, although it is still evident that noble titles impress many men and women today with typically servile attitudes.

But nowadays the plutocracy, the 'aristocracy of wealth', the big bank account, have become more influential. If someone has a lot of money at his disposal he lets it be known by his self-important behaviour, while the have-nots often betray their condition by a self-abasing attitude, unless they over-compensate by boasting.

If this sort of materialism belongs to the lower, physical level, then intellectualism belongs to the level above it, but is every bit as destructive. Intellectualism means excessive emphasis on intelligence and rationality. Parents cannot receive a greater compliment than praise of their children's intelligence. And the worst thing that could happen to them would be to doubt their children's intelligence. But intellect is only one aspect of an individual, even though it is an incredibly overvalued one. The price we pay for intellectualism is that authentic spirituality becomes that much more difficult to achieve.

Other, related prejudices are egotism and the need for admiration, both of which are theoretically regarded as wrong. A little story by Chuang-tzu shows how old this insight is. A Chinese emperor was once visited by a wood carver who had made a clock-stand that was immeasurably beautiful and astonished everyone who saw it. 'How can this be?' asked the emperor. 'You're only a simple wood carver, how could you produce such a marvel?'

'I don't know,' said the craftsman. 'But when I undertook to carve the stand I withdrew deep into my soul for three days. On the first day I forgot the fame it would bring me. On the second day I forgot the gold it would bring me. On the third day I forgot myself. After that, when I went into the forest and found the wood for the stand, I saw its shape so vividly in my mind's eye that I just had to free it from the wood. That's how I made the clock-stand.'

'What you're saying sounds so simple,' replied the emperor, 'but it's a great wonder nonetheless!'

This story is 2,500 years old, yet we cling to these prejudices still. The path from egotism to spirituality is called spiritualisation, a process which involves breaking free from prejudice and dedicating our entire lives to knowledge, love and faith.

Egotistical people mistrust their feelings, their bodies, their capabilities, their own natures and temperaments, life in general, success and other people. They want to be totally independent but they fear the responsibility freedom entails and, without even realising it, make themselves dependent on everything and everyone: science, medicine, psychology, the state, other people's opinions and so on.

The more egotistical a person is, the unhappier he feels in his heart of hearts, and so he seeks escape in pleasure and cheap thrills, whether nicotine, caffeine, sex, alcohol or drugs. Egotistical people are always afraid, even when they have learned to hide their anxiety behind a brave front. To put it another way, the less courage we have the more egocentric we are.

4

DEVELOPING
SELF-KNOWLEDGE

*'O My servants! Could ye apprehend with what wonders of
My munificence and bounty I have willed to entrust your souls,
ye would, of a truth, rid yourselves of attachments to all created
things, and would gain a true knowledge of your own selves—
a knowledge which is the same as the comprehension of Mine
Own Being.'*[25]

Courage

Before we can really develop ourselves we have to find out
how much courage we have. We usually have false ideas
about this because we do not want to admit our fears about
ourselves or other people. Even people who are considered
very courageous, certain sportsmen for example, can hardly
be absolutely fearless in today's world. We live in fearful
times, ours is a frightened generation. This is frequently
true of precisely these people who are considered especially
courageous—people who need to prove their courage to
themselves and others because they are full of fears. But
this should not mean that fear is an intrinsic part of the
human condition. Even today we can overcome our fears
to a great extent, if not completely. But first we have to be
brave enough to admit them to ourselves. In order to estab-

lish how afraid or—to put it more positively—how courageous we are, we must be clear about what we mean by 'courage'.

Courage does not mean the heroic posturing of the person who performs some risky deed or other; rather, it is a quality available to everyone. It is not a typically masculine attribute. Being courageous can mean the following:

1) Facing up to life's swings between joy and sorrow.
2) Standing up to even the greatest difficulty, looking at it critically and trying to overcome it. Overcoming obstacles is one of the most important tasks in life.
3) Taking responsibility for one's actions and accepting their consequences. This is part of what we mean by 'personal courage' or having the courage of one's convictions, and has nothing to do with masculinity or femininity.
4) Tolerating criticism. This is really not easy, because we tend to become defensive straight away.
5) Admitting one's mistakes without feeling humiliated. Many people are prepared to admit their mistakes and failures, even to other people, but they usually feel humiliated in doing so. Only when we overcome this feeling of humiliation by accepting that nobody is perfect and everybody makes mistakes can we claim to be even reasonably courageous.
6) Being flexible. This means that one is adaptable and sensitive to the situations and conditions at hand—one of the most important aspects of personal development.
7) Being prepared to make oneself unpopular if necessary. We should not simply conform or go along with the group; we ought to have a more idealistic view of solidarity than that. If the group in which we find ourselves does not move in the right direction, we should even

70

risk making ourselves disliked in order to help the group develop and make the right sort of progress.

8) Being able to cope by oneself, without always having to burden others with one's affairs.

9) Feeling responsible for the social ramifications of one's actions.

Of course this is not an exhaustive discussion of what it means to be courageous, but this list can give us some idea of the state of our own inner courage and self-confidence.

Social awareness

'Let your vision be world-embracing, rather than confined to your own self.'[26]

Social awareness, like courage, is an important gauge of our current state of personal development. Social awareness means consideration for others, objectivity, logical thinking, readiness for action, and above all a willingness to take responsibility. According to Adler social awareness (or 'social interest' as it is sometimes referred to), is the most important attribute an individual brings with him into the world. But it must be developed. In early childhood it is often, of course, the mother who is responsible for this. Social awareness is the basis of normal adjustment; to be socially aware means to be positive and helpful, to pursue one's own interests without losing interest in other people and their interests. The greater a person's social awareness the smaller his feeling of inferiority, and the greater his courage and self-confidence, optimism and feeling of being at home in life. Nothing makes a person feel his existence is justified and worthwhile so much as knowing he can be of use to others.

Having social awareness means having trust, seeing a purpose to life and not always yearning for security. We are not on this earth to be secure. But it does not mean simply being extrovert, adapting at any price, merely participating in some group. It means following a goal of perfection and wanting to help others develop themselves also.

The more equal one feels, the more social awareness one has. We could even say that social awareness is the yardstick of so-called 'normality'. Harmonious social relationships depend upon social awareness. Social awareness increases tolerance, and the ability to cooperate is an important criterion of social awareness. The less cooperation a person is prepared to give, the more he or she betrays an undeveloped sense of social awareness.

The development of social awareness requires positive self-assessment which, as we shall see, is possible if we are prepared to be positive about ourselves. This can be quite an objective exercise which has nothing to do with self-praise since no individual is completely without positive aspects.

The family constellation

'The integrity of the family bond must be constantly considered, and the rights of the individual members must not be transgressed . . . All these rights and prerogatives must be conserved, yet the unity of the family must be sustained.'[27]

Understanding the family constellation and its effects is vital for self-knowledge; it makes us aware of the different influences that have formed us within the family as children, depending on whether we grew up as an only child, a middle child or a youngest child. These influences do not control us absolutely, but they can impel us to move in certain directions in life. The possibilities, obstacles and challenges we encounter, our expectations and disappointments, success or lack of success are strongly influenced by

72

our position in the order of siblings in our family. The influences and experiences within the family form a frame of reference through which a child understands the world outside the family as well. The extent to which a child believes she can turn her abilities into accomplishments at home influences her ability to cope with situations outside the home.

Accordingly we can understand a child's character as an expression of what takes place within the family group, instead of attributing his character formation chiefly to heredity, emotional-sexual development or external stimuli. The family constellation must be regarded as something dynamic; furthermore, we must recognise that a child is influenced not only by family circumstances but also by her own interpretation of them and by the mutual influences within the social sphere we call the family. In her efforts to belong, to achieve a place in the family group, a child develops her own personal strategies in her early relationships with other family members and prompts them to treat her the way she expects them to.

Different children react quite differently to the same situation, so that in no family do two children, even identical twins, grow up in exactly the same situation. The family environment is different for each individual child. And obviously the birth of each subsequent child changes the situation. We must also remember that parents become older and more experienced with each new child. They may become sufficiently better off to own their own home. Or they may become poorer through some misfortune. Or perhaps they may move to another area where the neighbours are different. Another factor which may alter the situation is the arrival of step-parents because of divorce or death.

Another important factor is whether a sibling is ill or crippled, or whether a child is born shortly before or after the death of another child. Being an only boy among girls is a special situation, as is being an only girl among boys. Even certain obvious physical characteristics, such as a child's prettiness, can exert strong influences. And we must take into account whether other people besides the nuclear family—the parents and children—also live in the house, grandparents for example, or aunts, lodgers or household help.

It is extremely important to establish whether the parents preferred a child to his siblings in any way. Nothing is so discouraging in early childhood as the belief that a child's siblings are preferred to himself. Even today boys are often still allowed to assume superior or special roles which can give their sisters inferiority complexes. Children are exceptionally good observers, but they cannot always interpret what they observe correctly, so that merely the suspicion that others are preferred to himself or herself can cause a child to develop in the wrong direction. Now let's look at some typical family constellations.

The only child
The only child spends his entire childhood among grownups who know and can do more than he right from the start. Because of this it may be important for him to earn their recognition, so he might distinguish himself by developing the skills necessary to do this. But he might also decide to appeal to their sympathy and develop a tendency towards shyness, timidity or helplessness.

The only child is usually a spoiled child. If a boy, he will often have a mother complex, that is, he will grow up very dependent on his mother. In his adulthood this may influence him to the extent that, when choosing a partner, he looks for a woman who can replace his mother. A boy may also feel that his father is his rival. This circumstance, however, should not be specifically associated with sexu-

74

ality. It often happens that the father, who has thus far had the mother completely to himself, becomes jealous when the first child is born because so much of his wife's time is taken up with the baby whereas before she could devote it all to her husband.

An only child often enjoys her position as the centre of attention of a smaller or larger circle of adults and is usually strongly interested in her own person. Parents are generally more anxious about their first child than they are about the later ones, so only children often show signs of feeling insecure. Frequently only children have not learned to achieve things by themselves but instead exploit other people and expect to receive everything the instant they want it. If these expectations are not met the child can feel hard done by and refuse to cooperate. It must be emphasised that these and subsequent comments do not necessarily indicate how things always develop, but rather describe possible developments which have often been observed.

The first child
The first child frequently enjoys a privileged position; he or she was, at least for a time, the only child and therefore the centre of attention. Such children may come to think that they always have to be first. From then on they always try to retain some kind of superiority over the subsequent children. When the second child is born the first child often feels dethroned, and may consequently be discouraged and refuse to assume any responsibilities. He believes he's neglected rather than loved and so strives to retain or win back his mother's attention and service by positive achievements. Should this fail he turns idle and becomes a nuisance. If his parents then get into conflict with him he can become a problem child.

The first child may develop an especially capable, positive pattern of behaviour or she may be deeply discouraged. In her struggle to retain the upper hand she sometimes makes the effort to protect and help others. Not infrequently she may express hatred and even death wishes toward the second child. If the first child is a boy and a sister follows soon after, the personal conflict between them may be the basis of later sexual dissatisfaction. Between the ages of one and seventeen girls generally develop more quickly than boys. The first-born boy may thus be overtaken by his little sister. Then, usually exploiting the still common social preference for boys, he attempts to assert his position and take advantage of his masculine role. A girl, on the other hand, may develop an inferiority complex in response to her feminine role and press forward in a form of over-compensation.

The second child
The second child occupies a rather uncomfortable position and often behaves something like a locomotive. She is constantly under pressure, and tries to catch up with the older child in order to avoid this constant pressure from him. A second child never has her parents' undivided attention but always has another child ahead of her who is generally more advanced. If she believes she cannot win against the first child her claim to equality is questioned. These children often behave as if they were in a race, being overactive and pushy. We almost always observe competition between the first two children which suggests that their characters will develop in contrasting ways. If one child is reliable and good, the other may become unreliable and bad. If one is successful, the second will probably feel insecure and doubt his own abilities. If a third child is born the second becomes caught in between, a so-called 'sandwich child'.

76

The middle child of three
This child has an insecure place within the family group and often feels neglected, for he discovers that he has neither the privileges of the youngest nor the rights of the oldest child. Consequently he may feel unloved and abused and become convinced that the world is unfair to him. He may then not be able to find a place in the group, which can discourage him very deeply and make him a difficult child, a problem child.

If children are in the middle of larger families they normally develop more stable characters. Even sibling rivalry is usually less pronounced. Generally the larger the family, the less conflict and rivalry there is among the children.

The youngest child
Depending on the age differences between herself and her other siblings, the youngest child is often like an only child. Frequently everything is done for her: her decisions made and responsibilities assumed by others. Usually spoiled by the entire family these children become Super Babies with several 'mothers and fathers' if older siblings also assume parental roles. As the smallest and weakest child the youngest finds herself in an awkward situation and is often not taken seriously by the other siblings. But she may also become the 'boss' of the family, in that she develops into a winner because she feels left so far behind. In this case she tries to outdo all her older siblings and become the most successful. Conversely she may develop an inferiority complex and avoid a direct struggle for superiority. Perhaps she may retain the 'baby' role, manipulating others to help her and thereby making a strength out of weakness. Perhaps she may form a bond with the oldest child since both stand at either end of, and thus somewhat outside, a row.

77

Generally it can be said that siblings who exhibit great differences in character, temperament, interests, abilities and so forth probably grow up as competitors, while those with similar character traits tend to form alliances. We must distinguish here between competition and rivalry. Competition is fundamental and deep-seated, leading to differences in character, while rivalry is superficial, merely seeking an immediate, direct equalisation through conflict. Rivals—children, that is—who quarrel a lot are not necessarily competitors. On the other hand competitors may renounce all rivalry in that one child is the leader, the active one, the protector on whom the other one depends and from whom he receives support on account of his weakness and inferior position.

If there is a very great age difference between children each child may display the characteristics of an only child. Greater age differences may also result in groupings within the family, so that, depending on the number of children, two or more family groups exist within the one family.

It is important for our personal development that we recognise all these childhood influences. A child uses his situation and perceptions to evolve his own life pattern, way of interacting and characteristic traits.

If, incidentally, very pronounced similarities exist among children of the same family, these may be attributed to the family atmosphere. The family atmosphere, as distinct from the family constellation, frequently depends more on the parents: their attitudes, their goals in development and their system of values.

It is important for our self-knowledge that we identify the person with whom we were competing while growing up. It used to be thought that an age difference of six to seven years was sufficient to rule out competition between two children. The older child felt so superior that she did not regard the younger child as a competitor. Nowadays, however, when there is so much anxiety, and competition is on the increase, we may observe that even an age difference of ten years does not prevent children from competing with one another.

Early childhood memories

Before you read any further, please write down your earliest childhood memories. What matters is not so much the content, but that the memories are as early as possible, that they stretch as far back as you can remember. If possible, write down your five earliest memories. If you have more memories from this period, that is, from your pre-school years, you do not have to write down more than five. But if you have trouble remembering this far back, you should at least write down three memories. In noting down these memories it is important to distinguish between memory and story. If you remember that on Sundays you always went walking with your grandfather, this is not really a memory but a story, involving something which was known to happen repeatedly. But if you go further and say that such-and-such a thing happened on one of these walks, this event probably does represent a real memory.

Our earliest childhood memories are the best way of ascertaining our own life pattern. Such memories are the expression of a small child's most basic attitudes. If out of the many thousand experiences of early childhood only these few have remained in our memory, it's because they were of special significance and correspond to the picture we formed as a small child of the world, of other people, life in general and of ourselves. To some extent our earliest memories offer us the opportunity to recognise our own long term goals, of which we are normally unaware or insufficiently aware. Experience has shown that a person's earliest memories interrelate. Differences or contradictions between them are usually superficial.

If someone has no early childhood memories this is usually a person who does not want to look into himself. If someone has only pleasant memories, it may be the case that no other people appear in them at all, which suggests that as a child the person experienced his surroundings as unpleasant and built up his own world as a replacement. It might also be the case, however, that someone has pleasant memories only because they contrast with real life, which has never again been as pleasant as it was in his memory. In this way a person confirms his own negative impression of life.

The role a person herself plays in her childhood memories is also important. If she was active then, she will probably be active later in life too. If, on the other hand, she is only a passive observer, she will be more likely to assume the role of spectator in later life too. If we achieve something in our early childhood memories we are more likely to be adventurous than if we achieve nothing or fail at something.

If we are alone and mention no one else this may mean that we have had bad experiences with others as a child and are consequently afraid of cultivating close contacts with people. If, on the other hand, we are with other people, then later, too, we will probably be more sociable. If one's mother is remembered in a relatively positive role it is very likely she was an indulgent mother. We must also ascertain whether other people are remembered in a positive light, which would indicate that the child's social interest was well developed, or whether they behave negatively in one's memories, which would indicate that the child experienced his or her surroundings as hostile and still becomes irritated today at how bad the world is.

If someone appears who helps the child, this conceals

the other's feeling of helplessness. He believes he must rely on others' help. If his mother is not mentioned at all, the person probably feels that he was neglected as a child. If a person remembers being together with younger siblings this frequently indicates that he or she has felt dethroned by them. But it may also mean the person feels right only when associating with people weaker than himself. A memory of the birth of a younger sibling almost always indicates a feeling of having been dethroned.

A frequent memory is that of a holiday with one's mother, for example, or a memory of parents and grandparents in a friendly atmosphere. This may mean that the person prefers these people, thereby excluding others. Memories of dangers, accidents or beating generally indicate a emphasis on the hostile side of life. Memories of atrocities, thefts or sexual experiences often reveal a person's efforts to continue shutting these out of his or her life. The memory of sickness or death indicates fear of these things and is frequently associated with the desire to be a doctor or member of a caring profession in order to be better armed against them. The first day of kindergarten or school is another common memory, indicating that new situations generally make a big impression.

The symbolism in these early childhood memories is also interesting. Is the child above or below? If objects or other people are depicted as large or even gigantic, children have perceived themselves as concommittantly small. A marked degree of such symbolism, incidentally, indicates certain artistic gifts. It is also possible to discover visual, acoustical or motor tendencies in these earliest memories, which show that a person relies more on his eyes, his ears or his muscles respectively. Incidentally, childhood dreams, that is, the memory of dreams one had in one's pre-school years, have the same significance as childhood memories.

It is of great importance for personal development to

ascertain which long term goals one is pursuing in life. If one is always at the forefront, always playing the major role, one's long term goal is probably always to be first. If one does not succeed in this by doing good, then one may try to be first in trivial matters. Such a person lives 'on his nerves' and makes a nuisance of himself. Yet another goal is that of pleasing others. The desire to be good is often observed in first- or second-born girls who have grown up competing with a brother. Still other people are mainly concerned with achieving recognition. The long term goal of arousing other people's sympathy is also common. Often someone is convinced he must be special. If a person wants to be special, this manifests itself in childhood memories through the quite special quality of his experiences and the role he played in them. 'I must not make any mistakes.' 'I have to be right.' 'I must have everything under control.' These are typical examples of life patterns which show clearly through one's childhood memories.

The above remarks should enable anyone to discover at least a few aspects of his or her personal life pattern. Of course it is not possible to discover one's entire life pattern alone, without outside help. But it can begin to help a good deal if a person becomes clearer about some aspects of it.

It would be appropriate here to explain the concept of 'life pattern' more fully. Life pattern refers to the view small children form unconsciously on the basis of their experiences of life, of the world, of other people, of themselves and of their own qualities and abilities. This child's-eye view is not necessarily correct. Children are exceptionally good observers, but they do not have enough knowledge or experience to be able to interpret correctly what has happened in their lives, so their life patterns always contain errors. Most people go to their graves with the same life pattern they formed in early childhood. Even as adults we cannot correct the errors in our life patterns, because we are not aware of them. Adjustments to our life pattern can really be made only through therapeutic treatment or counselling, so part of us always remains a small child. There is one other way of changing our life pattern, but one we generally cannot count on. Sometimes particularly drastic experiences, usually of a religious nature, can shake us so fundamentally that aspects of our life pattern are changed. What we may hope to achieve, what we can achieve through personal development, is to recognise certain aspects of our life pattern and change them using the techniques to be discussed later.

Dreams

'That truth is often imparted through dreams no one who is familiar with history, and especially religious history, can doubt. At the same time dreams and visions are always coloured and influenced more or less by the mind of the dreamer and we must beware of attaching too much importance to them. The purer and more free from prejudice and desire our hearts and minds become, the more likely is it that our dreams will convey reliable truth, but if we have strong prejudices, personal likings and aversions, bad feelings or evil motives, these will warp and distort any inspirational impression that comes to us.'[28]

Dreams can also foster self-awareness but, like our earliest memories, they can only be partially understood without outside help. Essentially it is not the dream but the dreamer which needs to be interpreted. There are, however, certain typical or universal dreams which tend to occur again and again in which we can discern a number of characteristic elements. They include the following:

Anxiety dreams often indicate that the dreamer tends to

exaggerate the hostility of the world or other people, of life, reality or fate. Dreams usually prepare the dreamer for the next day, so anxiety dreams suggest that a person is unconsciously resorting to a form of avoidance behaviour, conjuring up feelings of anxiety which effectively keep him from doing something he really ought to do. Of course this is only one of many possible interpretations.

Flying dreams often indicate a wish to 'move upwards'. They are frequently dreams of ambition. The dreamer wishes to rise above others, to fly over others, to be able to do something that others cannot do, and so forth. Not infrequently flying dreams are coupled with

Falling dreams. These dreams, in which a person is falling, floating or hurtling downwards, are usually interpreted as compensatory. In the dream a person allows himself to fall, something he would not do in real life where his natural need for self-abandon is inhibited. People who do not really feel they belong, who do not feel at home anywhere, often experience such dreams.

Pursuit dreams are a kind of anxiety dream. It is important in these dreams to identify the pursuer(s). If the dreamer is pursued by other people, he or she believes them to be enemies with hostile intentions. If a woman dreams that men are pursuing her, this often indicates the so-called 'masculine protest'. (We shall consider an example of this in Chapter 8). Women who have this type of dream are usually worried about having to play an inferior gender role. If a dreamer is pursued by animals, this may express general anxiety about life, although often the animals, depending on their type (for example lions, tigers, dogs, etc.), can be interpreted symbolically. Being pursued by objects or by something undefinable may indicate general anxiety about life. Pursuit dreams are often coupled with

84

Hindrance dreams. In these dreams the person cannot run as he wants to, feels as if his feet are made of lead, or is unable to shout or call out. These dreams indicate that the dreamer feels impeded in life. He has insufficient confidence in himself and his abilities.

Embarrassment dreams. Usually in these dreams a person suddenly finds himself half-dressed or even completely naked in public, for example on the street. Frequently too the dreamer goes to the toilet only to find that he is not alone. In other words, one finds oneself in an embarrassing situation. These dreams indicate that a person fears showing his ignorance. He does not think very highly of himself and is very concerned to keep his presumed or actual inferiority secret, so other people do not notice how insignificant he really is.

Railway station dreams. These are dreams in which a person wants to catch a train, a bus, a ship, an aeroplane or some other mode of transport, and either barely makes it or just misses it. These dreamers fear coming off badly in life. If the person just makes the train it usually indicates a somewhat more confident attitude than if she has to watch it pulling out because she has arrived too late. Every trip on a bus, aeroplane or whatever, and even walking or riding on the street, can be equated with the journey through life. Does life run smoothly or do obstacles arise? Is one alone in the train compartment or with other people? Are there obstacles or accidents during the journey?

School and examination dreams. People who still dream about school after they have left often have trouble coming to terms with the past. Since dreams are essentially a preparation for what is to come, whether or not a person passed her exams or was successful at school in the dream is significant. The passed exam might indicate a wish for the

85

successful outcome of a project in reality. But it can also be a source of discouragement if a person is telling herself in the dream that passing an exam is no big deal, while in reality it is quite a different matter.

Sexual dreams. If married people have such dreams they could be interpreted as guidance in relation to their partners. Sexual dreams in single people, on the other hand, could be interpreted as preparation for marriage in general. A normal sex life will generally not produce sexual dreams.

Daydreams. These indicate pessimism. The role a person plays in a daydream is usually a role he believes himself incapable of playing in real life. The belief that one can realise one's ideals makes daydreaming unnecessary.

It must be emphasised that the content of a dream is not nearly as important as the mood or feelings it evokes. If a man dreams his wife has died and feels relieved when he wakes up and finds her sleeping peacefully beside him, naturally this dream has a different meaning than if he were to wake up and feel disappointed that she is still alive!

If someone dreams about something she experienced the previous day, these images are called 'remnants of the day'. In themselves they are less significant than is usually believed. Of greater significance is the use made of the remnants of the day in the dream. They are building blocks out of which the dreamer constructs, in her own random order, something which is independent of the character of the remnants themselves. In this her dream resembles real building. If a builder has stones delivered it is not possible to determine from the kind of stones they are what sort of house he wants to build. In the same way these dream building blocks, the remnants of the day, are less important than what the dreamer makes of them.

Problems and desires

'Our afflictions, tests and trials are sometimes blessings in disguise, as they teach us to have more faith and confidence in God, and bring us nearer to Him.'[29]

If we write down our present problems and difficulties and consider them in the light of what we've learned about ourselves so far, we can reach some fundamental conclusions. First one writes down at random everything that springs to mind. For example:

nervousness
lack of concentration
stomach pains
being unlucky in love
education problems
jealousy
indecision
temper tantrums
lack of will power
difficulty in relating to others
anxiety
guilt
incompetence
getting worked up too quickly
inability to say 'no'
lack of time
ambition
inferiority complex
learning disabilities
pessimism
impatience
inability to speak in public

insomnia
depression
apathy about work
fear of going bald
seeing no meaning to life
smoking too much
drinking too much
addiction to sweets
addiction to eating
lack of appetite
passivity
lack of self-assertion
procrastination
impatience
restlessness
stress
constipation
hypersensitivity
financial problems
being socially inept
dissatisfaction
being unable to plan
no sense of objectivity
lack of initiative

inclination to run away from things
stuttering
blushing
feeling inhibited
loneliness
shyness
bad temper
moods
lethargy
untidiness
unsatisfactory sex life
stubbornness
lack of openness
being sick and tired of housework
insecurity
breaking out in perspiration
indifference
feeling misunderstood
impulsiveness
nail biting
fear of the dark
inability to compromise
headaches
difficulty getting up
sensitivity to weather
self-pity

being over-idealistic
bad dreams
having no opinions of one's own
lack of confidence
not feeling free inside
inability to be silent
egotism
unpunctuality
lack of imagination
lack of persistence
fear of heights
palpitations
fear of illness
irritability
having negative thoughts
feeling empty inside
forgetfulness
inability to express oneself
always saying the wrong thing
tenseness
being easily influenced
having no faith
being one-track minded
fear of the opposite sex

This selection of common problems ought to show the range of things a person can come to grips with, helped by the personal development techniques explained in the next chapter. The spontaneous order in which we write down our personal problems gives some indication of how urgent a particular problem is. In other words, the problem listed first will be more upsetting than the one listed last.

The next step is to organise our list of problems by dividing them into external or physical problems and internal or emotional ones. Finally we must separate the problems we consider 'difficult' to solve from those that seem easier, because when we start working on them it is a good idea to begin with the 'easy' problems. We are thus more likely to succeed, which will encourage us to go on.

It is also appropriate to identify and analyse our desires in the same way, for they too can increase our self-knowledge by indicating the direction in which we're heading. Our desires are conscious goals and very often they contain the solutions to our problems. After having identified and categorised our desires, the final step is to devise a strategy for action, for without some sort of plan we shall never be able to realise our full potential for development.

5

THE PRINCIPAL TECHNIQUES
OF PERSONAL DEVELOPMENT

*'Take heed, O people, lest ye be of them that give good counsel
to others but forget to follow it themselves.'*[30]

The three main psychological methods of personal development described in this chapter are based on an understanding of the general principles, common prejudices and
self-knowledge discussed in previous chapters.

Making decisions

'Success or failure, gain or loss, must . . . depend upon
man's own exertions.'[31]

Human beings are decision-making creatures who determine every step they take themselves, even if this usually
does not happen on the conscious level (see Chapter 2).

Let's take an example. I am sitting at my desk and feel
a call of nature. So I go to the toilet. This may be a
conscious decision. But in order to put it into practice, I
make a host of unconscious decisions: I must decide to put
down my pen, push back my chair and exercise certain
groups of muscles in order to get up. I put my right foot

in front of my left—another decision—then my left foot in front of my right, open the door and so forth.

We make decisions without realising it consciously even more frequently in the emotional sphere than on the physical level. The following general technique was developed with this fact in mind. Let's illustrate it using insomnia as an example. A woman is lying in bed and suddenly realises that she has been lying there for quite a while without falling asleep. If she tells herself at this point that it's high time she fell asleep because she has to get up early for work tomorrow, and tries to force herself by saying, 'Look, you've really got to get to sleep now,' this will probably spell the onset of insomnia because by now she is in conflict with herself (see Chapter 3).

Before she can get anywhere she has to realise that she herself decides whether to sleep or not. It is her sleep. If she does not fall asleep, this means she does not want to fall asleep. Naturally this sounds paradoxical, because she believes it is in her own interest to fall asleep. But we must distinguish between the conscious, rational will and the unconscious will. If reason tells our insomniac she must now fall asleep, yet she does not do so, it must be assumed that her unconscious will is the stronger of the two. Since there is no point in fighting it, she must first of all accept her own decision not to fall asleep, in order to avoid this hopeless conflict with herself.

The next step is for her to realise that if she could choose insomnia, she can also choose sleep. To avoid conflict with herself she must distance herself from the situation by mentally stepping outside herself. So in her imagination she might sit on the chair next to the bed and watch herself lying there. By now she is no longer concerned with the problem of getting to sleep or not getting to sleep; instead she wants to determine objectively whether or not she wants to sleep (that is, whether her conscious or unconscious will

91

is stronger). If she manages that—and everyone can learn to do it—then it might just happen that she suddenly falls asleep.

This is how the process looks when we break it down into steps:

1) 'I'm still awake, which means I've decided not to fall asleep, since people do what they want to do.'
2) 'I have to accept this decision because nothing in the world can change it.'
3) 'But I could also decide to fall asleep.'
4) 'Now I'm going to step back and observe myself to find out what I really want: do I want to fall asleep, or do I want to stay awake?'

If this technique works, well and good. Our insomniac has fallen asleep. But if it has not worked, then the next step in the process begins:

5) 'Obviously I want to stay awake. But this is inconvenient. If I choose the uncomfortable, inconvenient option, it must be because this decision offers me some hidden advantage, such as the achievement of one of the five immediate goals.'

This makes sense because no one decides to do what is uncomfortable if he cannot anticipate certain advantages from it. This fifth step represents the transition from the first to the second technique, which is described below.

The first technique is a purely rational one and for this reason is often unsuccessful in cases involving deep-seated problems. This technique should always be tried in the first instance, however, and with practice a person can learn to do it in a split second. Even as a purely intellectual device it very often proves effective and in any case is a necessary preliminary for learning the following technique.

92

The five immediate goals

A person exhibiting anti-social behaviour is nearly always pursuing one of the five 'immediate goals'.[32] This assertion should in no way be taken as a simplification of emotional processes; if we are honest and courageous enough we can nearly always identify one of these five goals as the driving or, rather, attracting force motivating our problematical behaviour.

The five immediate goals are:

1) excusing one's own deficiencies
2) attracting attention
3) establishing superiority
4) retaliation
5) retreat

The second technique simply consists in identifying which of these five goals is motivating the behaviour in question. For example, if we realise which goal a particular bad mood is taking us towards, we can no longer abandon ourselves to this mood to the same extent as before. The main thing is to identify our immediate goal: nearly everything else will follow of its own accord. So now let's find out how to recognise these goals.

There are three ways to do this. We have already encountered the first way, which is to be familiar with the five goals and to use this familiarity to identify which goal is motivating our actions at any one time. But this is admittedly rather indefinite and usually necessitates a further step: predicting the consequences of the mood or behaviour in question. Once we have identified these consequences we are already quite close to recognising the goal. In general there are two types of consequences, personal and environmental. Predicting our own probable reactions represents the second way of identifying our immediate goal; recognising the probable consequences on our environment represents the third way.

A person can use his or her behaviour to pursue any one of the five goals. But just because we recognise a particular goal in one case, we cannot take it for granted that the next time we exhibit similar behaviour we shall be trying to achieve the same goal. For example, one time we could be trying to excuse our own shortcomings and the next time seeking revenge. Since the first technique was explained in terms of insomnia, let's continue with this example.

Let's say, then, that the night before a difficult examination a student tosses and turns without sleeping a wink. Secretly he is very doubtful about whether he will pass this exam and has a magnificent excuse prepared in case he does not: he can say that he would have done well if only he had been able to sleep the night before. In this case he has been using his insomnia to pursue goal 1. But perhaps he passes the examination. In this case it is easy for him to feel superior (that is, achieve goal 3), telling himself how terrific he is for passing this exam without even having had a good night's rest beforehand!

Or let's assume that a husband is in a bad mood the morning after a sleepless night and his wife is soothing and sympathetic. This man has probably been pursuing goal 2, since he receives more attention and solicitude from his wife than he otherwise could have expected. His wife might even say to the children, 'Daddy slept badly last night, so you must be especially nice and quiet today.' This might give the husband a feeling of superiority (and thus add goal 3 to his list of achievements) because the entire household is having to do what he wants. It is even possible that because of his insomnia and his consequent bad mood he starts a quarrel with his wife and makes life hell for her the entire day. He can excuse his behaviour to himself by saying it is not his fault that his insomnia has made him so

94

aggressive, when all along he actually wants to take revenge (goal 4) for something his wife did yesterday.

A familiar illustration of goal 5, retreat, is the man who escapes into his study or garage or takes refuge behind his newspaper or in front of the television when his more talkative wife wants to have a conversation.

The technique discussed in this section cannot be applied in the same way in every instance. For example, if we are very irritable or angry we can hardly sit down quietly and patiently go through the possible consequences of our behaviour. In this situation it is advisable to use the technique later, since it will always be good training for the next time. Once our irritation or anger has subsided we can consider which of the five goals we wanted to attain with it. This subsequent application of the technique is necessary to enable us to go through the mental exercise more and more quickly. The aim is to be so at home with this technique that it only takes a split second to realise which goal we are unconsciously pursuing, so that we do not always fall into our habitual patterns of behaviour. Thus when we find ourselves in a situation in which we normally become very irritated we can succeed in recognising our goal before the irritation completely takes over. In this way we can learn to pre-empt our irritation.

Life pattern as a technique

Suppose a man is aware of one aspect of his life pattern, for instance he believes he is over-dependent on help from others. To continue with the example of insomnia: if after a sleepless night he asks his wife to help him with chores he normally would have done by himself, that aspect of his life pattern would be responsible for his insomnia. But even when he realises this—when he tells himself 'I depend too much on others' help' and connects this with his

95

insomnia—nothing changes. Clearly his insomnia is more deeply rooted than that, and he cannot expect an immediate improvement just because he has become aware of this aspect of his life pattern. It is typical of this third technique of personal development that we must practise it before we see results. We must be constantly aware of which aspect of our life pattern is involved in our neurotic behaviour.

In time this rational process will be translated into action, in that we will have trained ourselves to become angry with ourselves or with the 'little guy' in us. This anger represents a phase in the application of this technique which we absolutely must get through. If we succeed, after more practice we will reach a different stage where instead of becoming angry with ourselves over a particular aspect of our life pattern, we begin to find it amusing. It then strikes us as funny that the little guy still wields so much power. From the moment when we no longer take him so seriously a far-reaching change can take place. From then on (to continue with the above example) the insomniac will believe less and less that he is so totally dependent on help from others.

Without professional guidance we will never be in the position to understand our entire life pattern, but we can still achieve a very great deal if we recognise some aspects of it.

If a person's sleeplessness is so ingrained and well-reinforced that it cannot be overcome with techniques 1 and 2, it should be possible to improve it using technique 3.

While the first technique can offer immediate results and the second technique may sometimes do so, working with the third technique requires decidedly more time and patience. How quickly results are achieved with technique 3 depends on how consistently all three techniques are practised. Chapter 8 gives some examples of how typical neuroses can be worked through using these three techniques. Everyone can learn something from reading through them. In general the techniques should be tried in the order in which they have been discussed in this chapter.

Here are some typical aspects of modern life patterns:

— I'm only a girl.
— Nature hasn't equipped me very well.
— I'm a little boy inside and can't imagine myself becoming a grown man.
— I don't have much self-confidence.
— I don't have all that much to offer.
— I need to depend on others.
— I must secure support, help and protection from others.
— I need sympathy from other people.
— I must achieve recognition.
— I want to be first.
— I want to be the centre of attention.
— I must please people.
— I must be good.
— I must have everything under control.
— I must be intellectually superior.
— I must be right.
— I mustn't make any mistakes.
— A strong husband/a good wife must look after me.
— I am special.
— I want to be special.
— I must let myself be persecuted so I can look down on my persecutors (martyr complex).
— I must be master of every situation.
— You can't depend on people.
— People are evil and unjust.
— Life is difficult and dangerous.
— I can't bear people to think badly of me.
— I have to be careful my freedom isn't limited.

— I'm unlucky.
— I want to assert myself and put my spouse in his or her place.

6

ADOPTING A POSITIVE OUTLOOK

'To look always at the good and not at the bad. If a man has ten good qualities and one bad one, to look at the ten and forget the one; and if a man has ten bad qualities and one good one, to look at the one and forget the ten.'[33]

This chapter is intended not as a description of another personal technique but as a discussion of basic attitudes which complement the three personal development techniques outlined in Chapter 5.

The positive

Try to see the positive and overlook the negative
This maxim is intended to reverse the failure mentality of our age and culture. It is up to individuals to decide whether they choose to see the positive or the negative. Things have no significance in themselves; it is the individual who gives a thing its significance. Let's say that I offer someone a book at £5; he could say that he is not at all interested in this book and would not even be prepared to pay 50p for it. But a friend sitting next to him sees the book and says he would gladly pay £7.50 for it since he has been looking for this particular book for years.

99

Things have significance only when an individual gives them significance. In this respect individuals have enormous importance, because they assign or choose not to assign significance to everything, even God. If an individual attributes no significance to God then God does not exist for him. But if he does attribute significance to God, then he gives God the power to influence him.

It is up to us whether we see a person's positive or negative side. Both are always present. As we have already seen in the discussion of optimism and pessimism, however, it is always worth concentrating on the positive. We can only build on the positive: it is impossible to build on the negative. A little girl comes home from school and her father asks to see her exercise book. The father usually scolds his daughter if her handwriting is poor; yet this will result not in the improvement of her handwriting but only in the child's further discouragement. This example was chosen in order to show how imperative it is to try to discover the good which may not be obvious at the outset. The father who really wants to help his child write better must first find something positive to say about her handwriting.

First he must look for a word his daughter has written well. If the writing is so poor that not a single word is well done, perhaps he can find a letter that looks good. If the father points out to the little girl a good small 'a' she has written, a very different process takes place in the child from when she only has her mistakes pointed out to her. When the latter happens she only hears her own suspicions of her inadequacy confirmed; she gets discouraged and does not write any better because she is convinced that she cannot learn to write well. But if her father points out the letters she has written well, then the child tells herself that she can write other letters equally well. She is encouraged by this and her self-confidence increases. If not even a single letter is properly written, however, the father can surely find at least an 'i' that is correctly dotted if he makes the effort. He must draw attention to this, because a child can only be encouraged by and build on the positive.

This example was intended to demonstrate that we generally see things far too negatively and to show how we must sometimes make a real effort to find at least one positive thing, however small it may be. We might take this example still further and suggest to the father that at least he can praise the child's efforts to write at all if he cannot even find a properly-dotted 'i'.

Expect the positive, but put yourself in neutral
We have already discussed the power of expectation so it should already be clear that we attract the positive by expecting it and in so doing we foster success. But the second part of the saying above is also important, because if we ignore it we can all too easily feel disappointed if the good we expected does not occur. 'To put ourselves in neutral' means that we should not hanker after success. Success is so overrated these days; yet we must be aware that we are not in this world always to be successful. Of course things can go wrong, of course the negative gets the upper hand sometimes, but this must not cause us to stir up negative feelings of disappointment within ourselves. Failure, too, is part of life; the main thing is that we know that next time we have another good chance to succeed by expecting the positive.

Conceal your own good deed, but reveal the bad one
Usually we do just the opposite. We are gratified when our good deed is observed, especially when we don't shout it from the rooftops. But if we publicise our own good deed, then, as the Bible says, 'We have our reward', that is, our action is recognised by other people, and this recognition

itself is our reward. This quotation is from the story in the Gospel of St Matthew about the man who prays, fasts and gives alms, but in an ostentatious way. His reward for these things lies in the knowledge that other people consider him a pious man. But if we behave like this we fail to accumulate anything good within ourselves, but immediately let it leak out again. Keeping a good deed secret, however, is like paying money into a bank account in order to accumulate credit. The moment we conceal a good deed the good remains in us and we become ever more positive and able to continue doing good, because people become the qualities they keep inside themselves.

Most people conceal the bad things they do because they are ashamed or because they believe other people's opinion of them will diminish. What they fail to realise is that by doing this they are accumulating negative things within themselves: shame, guilt—in short, a negative bank balance. The more we conceal our own faults and misdeeds, the more negative we become and the less capable of doing good in the future. This is why it is advisable to admit misdeeds and mistakes, though not of course in such a way as to degrade ourselves in front of others. The moment we admit a mistake we release the bad: it does not fester in us, making us even more negative. In other words, we must not conceal the bad, the cheap, the vulgar, the wrong, the erroneous, the stupid or the cowardly things we do, because then we become inwardly negative, insecure, anxious, pessimistic, miserable, apathetic, unproductive, insincere—indeed neurotic and morally and spiritually bankrupt—and we see neither joy nor meaning in life; perhaps we even hate ourselves.

Conversely we should not flaunt our good works and deeds, our virtues and strengths, for the 'credit' we amass by concealing them makes us more positive, optimistic, courageous, alive and creative; it enables us to accept

102

ourselves and gives us even more faith and confidence in ourselves and in other people.

Our actions

'Let deeds, not words, be your adorning.'[34]

Cultivate consistency between word and deed
This is an age-old problem. Whatever we say remains insignificant and ineffectual if our actions are inconsistent with our words. We only come across as credible, trustworthy and authentic when what we do agrees with what we say. The potential for personal development in this issue lies in our being accountable to ourselves for our own consistency, for our integrity. It probably does not need to be emphasised how important such consistency is in bringing up children as well.

Distinguish between deed and doer
When a child does something wrong his parents often scold him in a way that unintentionally makes him feel that he is not only naughty but also unloved. Distinguishing between the deed and the doer means being able to express complete disapproval of a person's reprehensible conduct without disapproving of the person himself, our fellow human being, our equal. Whatever a person does, he is still our fellow human being and retains his value as such. To disapprove of the bad deed, but never of the person behind it, requires tact and sensitivity. Only when we learn to make this distinction between the action and the actor does our ability to show love and encouragement to other people, even to strangers, increase.

There are several other ways of thinking which can also turn our attitude in a more positive direction. They should never originate from a feeling of superiority, however, because the moment we place ourselves above other people we become unable to help them. If someone has done something bad we must take into consideration what kind of person he is. Is he ignorant, or childish, or ill? If he is ignorant we should not get angry with him but instead recognise our responsibility to help him acquire more knowledge. If he is childish—that is, insufficiently advanced in his development—then we have just as little right to get angry with him as we would with a child. Our attitude should be one of understanding and willingness to help him in his development. Nor must we become angry with a sick person because he is sick. And if an emotional illness is behind his bad deed it is our responsibility to help him towards greater health, which is often possible through nothing more than an attitude of encouragement.

If we bear these things in mind we can steer human relationships in a more positive direction through increased goodwill and greater love.

What can I do?

This question implies that it is almost always inappropriate to expect someone else to take the first step. In every conflict, with whomever it may be, we must ask ourselves what we can do and not what the other person should do. As long as one person waits for the other to take the first step, this first step will usually be taken reluctantly or not at all.

Act, do not react

An animal reacts to stimuli from its internal or external environment. A person, of course, can also react, but it is more important for him or her to act, to do something positive. As long as we only react to something or someone else we make ourselves dependent. Only through an action which we ourselves have chosen can we be free to move as we should in the right direction, to do the right thing.[35]

Become more objective, but be aware that facts and causes are secondary
Being more objective means trying to judge things as they really are. The more objective we are the more likely we are to be able to avoid succumbing to prejudice. But here, too, it is important for us not to be perfectionists. Perfection is an unattainable goal, yet one which always points the way. If we were to become 100% objective we would probably no longer be able to make decisions or to act at all. We would see everything from all sides and would be able to judge which point of view was more important or more correct. A subjective assessment of the facts, then, is necessary; it should simply not be taken so far that we become unobjective. Subjectivity and objectivity are not mutually exclusive. What is important is that we use our common sense.

As we have already seen in Chapter 3, we usually attribute too much importance to facts. Our interpretation of the facts, however, and the way in which we use them, are more important than the facts themselves. Human beings are adaptable and need not allow themselves to be controlled either by facts or by causes.

Professional therapists are well acquainted with cases of beautiful girls and women who come for treatment because they are deeply insecure. Although extremely beautiful, these women do not believe themselves to be attractive. One would think that a look in the mirror or the opinions of people around them would be enough to convince them. The fact of their own beauty counts for nothing, however, compared to their personal opinion, which may have been formed through competition with a sister, for example. The sister, both as a child and an adult, may not have been

105

nearly as beautiful as the patient, but she knew how to charm the people around her. She won everyone's hearts, and as a result the patient incorrectly concluded that her sister was beautiful while she herself was an ugly duckling.

Interestingly enough, the reverse can also happen. In Athens, for example, girls are brought up to believe that 'There are no ugly women.' This can result in girls with completely unprepossessing appearances being convinced that they exert a fatal attraction for men. And they actually do attract men, because they believe in their own appearance. This, incidentally, is the celebrated difference between beauty and sex appeal. Sex appeal, a combination of self-confidence and interest in the opposite sex, can even triumph over beauty.

These examples should illustrate the fact that however important facts and causes may be, we should never consider them so important that we allow ourselves to be controlled by them.

Our attitude to others

Do not compare yourself
This issue has already been discussed in Chapter 2, where we saw that comparing oneself with others is meaningless and leads us to waste our energy on the see-saw of inferiority/superiority rather than progress along the 'horizontal' line of personal development. (In considering the issue of personal comparison it is useful to bear in mind the distinction between the doer and the deed.) Refusing to compare oneself with others does not mean it is inappropriate to take some other person as a model. Nor is it necessarily inappropriate to compare achievements. But to compare oneself personally with someone else is not only meaningless but harmful as well.

Take the example of two neighbours. Both bought

similar plots of land at the same time, built similar houses and planted small gardens. One day A noticed that B had installed a television antenna on his roof, the first one in the neighbourhood. A, who habitually compared himself with B and was competing with him without really being aware of it, himself acquired a television soon after. He had now caught up with B again. But B's line of work somehow seemed to be more in keeping with the current economic trends, and his material success was soon manifested in other ways. Suddenly he was driving a big limousine, and his wife got a car too. Then he was able to acquire a neighbouring piece of land, enlarge his garden and build an extension on his house. A became more and more uneasy and struggled to be able to afford these things too. One day, however, when he was invited to one of B's flashy parties, he had to face the fact that he could never catch up with B. The guests admired Mrs B's clothes, the expensive furniture and the beautifully landscaped garden. The host cleverly dropped the names of important people he knew and let it be known where he had taken his wife on a recent holiday. A now had to admit to himself that he could not compete but he still kept comparing himself with B. And so he too began to brag about everything under the sun without having anything concrete to back it up with.

If A had stopped comparing himself with B he could have freed himself from B's materialism and need for admiration and have developed his own inner values. We must not confuse this policy with 'sour grapes', however. We must realise that each individual is absolutely unique, something which has never existed before and will never exist again. To reiterate: the individual is a mine rich in gems of incalculable value. Each person's task is to bring these gems to light. But when we compare ourselves, we neglect our own personal development and instead toady to others, becoming totally dependent and servile. In such a situation, we are not able to concentrate on developing our own individual qualities and capacities, and these gems cannot come to light.

Neither quarrel (even with yourself) nor give in (even to yourself) but understand and try to help

This maxim has already been discussed in Chapter 3. Both quarrelling and giving in are equally inappropriate because the former offends the other person's dignity and the latter offends one's own dignity. Nothing can be achieved by quarrelling because quarrelling keeps breeding new quarrels. On the other hand people who give in for the sake of peace usually suppress their feelings so much that eventually they lead to a gigantic explosion.

A similar thing is true in getting along with oneself. It is not appropriate for people to try to control or master their feelings. This only throws them into inner conflict and they still do not succeed in accomplishing anything. It is equally inadvisable for people to give in to their feelings. If we allow our feelings free play it is more than likely that we will offend the dignity of others and lose their respect.

What is important is to try to understand others in the same way as we try to understand ourselves. The best way of doing this is to employ the second technique of personal development, the one connected with the five immediate goals. Once we have understood that we only get angry so we can tell someone off and thereby achieve a feeling of superiority, we not only understand ourselves better but can also help ourselves behave more appropriately. The same is true for others. Once we understand, for example, that a person only behaves badly towards us because he wants to feel superior, we also understand that behind all this striving for superiority is a person who feels weak and has very little self-confidence. Of course we could abuse this knowledge and turn it into a psychological weapon.

But making proper use of this knowledge would mean trying to help the other person in a way that allows him to accept our help.

We ought, then, to change the saying that 'The wiser person gives in' to 'The wiser person understands and helps,' but without priding ourselves on being the wiser person.

Forget the past

Of course this does not mean that we should ignore the past completely, but that we should forget it to the extent that we are likely to misuse it. If we have some beautiful memory, that is good. But obviously we can misuse this memory and adversely affect our functioning in the present by dwelling on the past. If we have bad memories it is important to realise this and learn from them, but then to stop looking back because this too can prevent us from behaving properly in the present. One common way of dwelling on the past is feeling guilty about something we have done wrong. We generally misunderstand our guilt feelings. Nietzsche said that guilt was unbecoming, and Dreikurs wrote, 'Guilt feelings are the expression of good intentions that we do not have at all.' The mechanism of guilt is quite different from what we usually believe.

Let's suppose that we have done something bad and have developed guilt feelings because of it. Naturally feeling guilty is unpleasant, and a bad conscience certainly does not help us sleep at night. So we tell ourselves (unconsciously of course), 'I've done something wrong, but I've made up for it because I'm suffering these pangs of conscience.' (We often pride ourselves on this by telling ourselves that at least we feel guilty, whereas other people are not even aware of their faults. Naturally we are unaware that we unconsciously acquire a feeling of superiority from this.) By feeling guilty we have, so to speak, punished ourselves for the wrong deed. In so doing we cancel our debt, and on the next occasion we will commit the same offence again. Our guilt feelings actually prevent us from improving, from truly repenting.

The same is true of self-reproach. A person who reproaches herself for a past action treats herself the way a bad teacher treats his pupils. Self-reproach discourages us, and thereby hinders us from doing what is right. It is important to recognise our past mistakes and then to undertake to minimise the same mistakes next time (see the next section).

As important and desirable as it might be to decide the morality of matters in a group context, that is, in society, it is psychologically undesirable to administer justice in the interaction between individuals, so long as love and agreement exist. As the example of the conflict between husband and wife on p. 61 indicates, interpersonal justice should serve people and help them to live together peacefully. To make oneself or anyone else the slave of justice is just as improper as to abuse justice to raise oneself above other people.

Our attitude to ourselves

Do not try to avoid mistakes, but minimise the ones you make
To err is human. As long as we attempt to avoid mistakes completely we discourage ourselves, because we cannot do it. We are fundamentally incapable of achieving perfection. So we need the courage to be imperfect.

Since we can never completely avoid mistakes it is advisable to adopt a policy of little steps. This means trying to make larger mistakes smaller. Let's say we have done something wrong, which is no reason to get angry. After all, we are only human. But next time we try to behave a bit better. These steps towards improvement should not be too big. If we attain the goal we set ourselves, namely to do something a bit better next time, we should try to regard this as a success. Only in this way is it possible to set a positive spiral in motion. The small success encourages us to achieve another success next time.

Forget the word 'must'

Many years ago I saw two pictures placed next to each other in an American psychology book. In one picture a crowd of children were dragging themselves with great effort through the snow. It was clear that they had been gathering wood in the forest which was visible in the background and were now reluctantly carrying it home. The second picture had the same children and the same landscape, but the children had loaded themselves down with twice as much wood and were happily singing and running home. The caption under the first picture ran, 'Children, today you must fetch wood!' Under the second picture the caption was, 'Children, today you may go into the forest and fetch wood!'[36] Naturally it is not sufficient simply to replace the word 'must' with the word 'may' in child-rearing but this illustration does give the right idea.

Generally we are extremely sensitive to the word 'must' because of educational methods that are still not democratic enough. No one gladly lets himself be ordered about. Orders should be replaced by suggestions. One should not give orders to oneself either. In the process of personal development we can actually make a 'may' out of each 'must' if we are prepared to see things in a positive light. In this way we free ourselves from the ordinary slave mentality of our time which makes us do many things only because we feel the 'must' behind them.

This mentality ensures that as soon as we wake up we face a struggle with ourselves. Many people think they are especially clever because they set their alarm clocks a few

111

minutes early and, thanks to this stratagem, 'enjoy' being able to stay in their cosy, warm beds a few moments longer before they set forth into the hostile world. But this only makes things more difficult for them. Getting up can be a pleasure if we see things positively and have positive expectations. Many people get up laboriously and sullenly every morning. Yet if they are on holiday they are so excited about the good time they are going to have that they happily get up even earlier than usual, possibly even jumping for joy! Life is full of examples of how dependent on external pressures we often make ourselves without really being aware of it. All the same it is not really so difficult to become more independent and to find inner freedom. The following example shows that this is possible even in difficult circumstances.

During the war a small group of soldiers in an exposed position were suddenly attacked by fighter-bombers. They threw themselves on the ground, which offered not the slightest protection, not a hillock, not a shrub, nothing. Bullets pelted the earth and the soldiers lay there overcome with fear, expecting to be hit at any moment. Only one of them was able to stop worrying about what was happening around him once he had realised that there was nothing he could do. But right in front of his nose he saw a tiny little plant growing and he took great joy in the tender, fresh green thing—it was March—and its delicate leaves. Outwardly he lay there exactly as the others did, but inwardly he made use of his inner freedom. At that moment he was not only free of fear but also free to experience joy.

Forget the words 'difficult', 'try' and 'hope'
When we are planning to do something challenging and keep imagining how difficult it will be, doing it becomes even more difficult. Anticipating the difficulty not only saps our energy but also diminishes our belief in success.

112

But if we start out with the attitude that life does have its difficulties but it doesn't pay to harbour or even express negative expectations, then we approach our projects more confidently. And this increases the chance of success.

A similar case is the use of the word 'try'. If the reader of this book tells herself that she will try to practise the techniques of personal development, she is already entertaining too many doubts which can damage the success of the techniques. She should not try to practise them, but instead simply apply herself to them without hankering after success right from the start. Every businesswoman must invest something before she can have a business. Before she can sell something she must have bought something. What we need is a small amount of starting-up capital in trust and faith.

The third word it is advisable to forget when planning something is 'hope'. Hope always implies a lack of faith. If we believe something, we are certain of it. 'Faith moves mountains.' To hope, on the other hand, means to be uncertain, to doubt. The positive power of expectation is greater if we believe than if we hope. As long as we can believe—and in personal development this should always be possible—we should be able to manage without hope.

7

DEDICATION TO LIFE'S TASKS

The three major tasks of an individual's life are occupation, love and marriage, and coexistence. We must hold our own in all three. If we do not succeed, it is probably because of some neurosis. Let's briefly discuss the tasks one by one.

Occupation

'It is incumbent on everyone to engage in crafts and professions, for therein lies the secret of wealth.'[37]

This is the task in which most people succeed one way or another, because failure can hardly be kept a secret from other people. Failing in either of the other two tasks, on the other hand, can usually be more or less successfully concealed.

The way in which we respond to this life task is closely associated with our attitude to it. Because of our antiquated methods of raising children, work is very often bound up with the word 'must'. Right from the start every small child wants to help his parents around the house. For example, he comes into the kitchen, where his father is busy with the washing-up. Naturally he wants to help, but his father is afraid he will break a dish. And he knows that his son's 'help' is not really a help to him at all; on the

114

contrary it takes up even more of his time. So he shoos the child away and discourages him with a remark such as, 'You can't do that yet, but when you're older. . .'

Then when the child is old enough to really be of use to his parents, he does not want to help any more. But he is forced to, he 'must'! And so the foundations of a wrong attitude to work are laid this early. This attitude is reinforced when a mother complains in her children's presence about the burden of housework, or comes home in the evening and is 'knocked out' by her day's work.

Theodor Mommsen once said, 'If a person no longer finds enjoyment in his work and only works in order to achieve pleasure as quickly as possible, then it is only by accident that he does not become a criminal.' And Voltaire wrote, 'Work keeps three great evils at bay: boredom, vice and need.' The higher the culture, the more highly work is regarded. It was Martin Luther who said: 'He who works faithfully prays twice.' According to Unamuno a person's occupation constitutes his true worship of God, so the true prayer of a shoemaker who believes in God lies in his making good shoes which prevent his fellow human beings from getting corns. In the newest religion, the Bahá'i Faith, work done in the right spirit is equated with the worship of God. In short, work should be not only a means of earning a living but also a *raison d'être*.

Love and marriage

Many people in our civilisation fail in this life task. A psychologist once rather waspishly stated that there were two kinds of marriage nowadays, the bad good marriage and the good bad marriage. In the former the partners often quarrel but always make up again, while in the latter the partners keep up outward appearances but actually have

115

nothing more to say to each other. They no longer live with each other, but alongside each other.

Naturally it is not that simple, but there are signs that point to an ongoing 'battle of the sexes'. One of these is the steadily increasing number of divorces. In West Germany around two hundred marriages now break up every day, while in the USA one divorce occurs every minute. Another sign is the number of children being born to single parents. In West Germany it is estimated that there are currently around one million children who were born to single mothers, while in the USA 350,000 such children are born every year, more than 40% of them to mothers between the ages of fifteen and nineteen. Young marriages, in which the husband or both partners are under twenty-one, may be regarded as another symptom. Of such marriages, 50% break up within five years. Cohabitation and partner swopping may also be indicative of attempts by discouraged people to find an acceptable solution to a life task which appears too difficult.

What do these unsatisfactory solutions stem from? Like all the difficulties of our age they stem from lack of faith. If a person has no faith in himself he cannot have faith in a partner. If a person has no faith in other people or in the community, he can have no faith in the community's laws and institutions either. However, monogamy represents the best solution to the life task of love and marriage, although today this may not be a universally popular view. Nevertheless, it has the greatest capacity to fulfil the deep yearning of each individual to feel that he or she belongs completely to another.

Another contemporary problem, ignorance of the difference between love and sex, is related to these other difficulties. Sexuality is only one element in love, an element which, as with other aspects of the human body, has its place on the animal level even though human sexuality

116

differs fundamentally from animal sexuality.[38] Sexuality should be at the service of love and not become an end in itself, in the service of purely physical sensations. Real love must be learned. Without courage and concern for others love is not possible. Bahá'u'lláh expressed this viewpoint in his famous essay, *The Four Valleys*: 'Love is a light that never dwelleth in a heart possessed by fear.'[39] Truly complete love between human beings always includes a spiritual element. Spirituality is the absence of egotism. 'Love is a force which kills the most poisonous weed in the human heart', wrote Gotthelf. Only a spiritual person can devote himself to it completely without losing his identity.

In contrast to young marriage there are several things to be said for early marriage, such as the greater adaptability of youth and consequently the increased potential for the partners to grow together; the vigour of youth; the increased social stability achieved by channelling sexuality into a permanent relationship; and the benefit to the extended family, especially the grandparents who live to see their grandchildren grow up. However, increasingly longer professional training often makes an early marriage difficult. Such marriages tend to have the greatest chance of success when the following conditions are met:

— Both partners should have a clear life-plan for their education and professions. Relationships with both sets of parents should be functioning well so that, on the one hand, the parents are prepared to continue giving not only emotional but also financial support if necessary, and, on the other hand, the young people are able to accept this help without feeling dependent or humiliated by it.
— There should be external order as to home, furniture, clothing and so on.
— Both partners should possess 'internal order', that is,

117

strength of character, patience, the ability to make sacrifices and to accept the partner's otherness, and independence from outside influences and prejudices.
— The other life tasks should be solved or at least on their way to being solved.

Marriage does not exist first and foremost to contribute to the solution of existing problems; rather it presents a new mutual task which can only be solved with a positive outlook and faith in oneself and one's partner. But even love can be misused. We need only think of so-called romantic love which nowadays, because it is overvalued, underlies so many relationships which eventually break up. Often it is merely the daydream of discouraged people who hope to use it to escape reality. Love can thus become a drug.

Romantic love is not a negative thing in itself, but only when nothing else is considered important, whether reason, common sense or the parents' opinions. It gets its apparent justification not only from profit-seeking and intellectually impoverished groups producing films, television, radio, newspapers and novels which glorify romantic love, but also from serious literature.

An example may be found in the words of Hugo von Hofmannsthal which Richard Strauss set to music in the opera *Arabella*: 'But the right man—if there is one for me in this world—will one day stand before me and will look at me and I at him, and there will be no doubts and no questions . . .'. Isn't it lovely to dream of such perfect romantic love; why shouldn't we give ourselves up to fantasies of this kind? But when we wake up from these daydreams we must switch our modern cognitive faculties back on. The 'right man for me' does not exist in this world; instead there are hundreds of thousands of members of the opposite sex who would suit us, if we were prepared to contribute, to assume responsibility, to adapt ourselves positively, to get the best out of our partner, to place our interests in his or her hands, and to be supportive.

'Trust and respect are the two inseparable cornerstones of love, without which it cannot exist', wrote Kleist. Trust and respect can only be achieved through social equality between women and men. At present this exists only in theory or on paper. In reality we still have a long way to go, even in the countries which are most progressive in this respect. Spiritually there are no differences between the sexes. 'Humanity is like a bird with two wings—the one is male, the other female. Unless both wings are strong and impelled by some common force, the bird cannot fly heavenward', commented 'Abdu'l-Bahá.[40]

Whether or not people are properly tuned in to their partners can be seen by whether they are more aware of their positive or negative sides. To find this out, take a paper and pencil and answer the following four questions. Note down the answers spontaneously, without stopping too long to think.

1) What do I appreciate in my partner, what do I like about him/her, what pleases me?
2) What complaints do I have about him/her, what annoys me about him/her, what don't I like so much?
3) What does my partner appreciate about me?
4) What complaints does he/she have about me?

Do not ask your partner for the answers to the last two questions; give what you believe to be the answers. When you have written down everything you can think of, compare the plus and minus points. Number them so you can see which are predominant. If your partner's positive aspects predominate, you have the right attitude. But if your partner ends up with more negative points it is high time you developed a more positive outlook. In any case you can work on all the negative points—especially your own of course—with the aid of the personal development techniques. If you do not understand what your partner likes about you at all, and perhaps have not given yourself any positive points, it is high time you used these techniques to work on your self-confidence.

Coexistence

'Nature in its essence is the embodiment of My name, the Maker, the Creator.'[41]

With nature
Human beings are part of creation: we are inseparably connected with it. Even if we regard ourselves as the pinnacle of creation, as creatures who cannot be circumscribed by nature, we are still dependent upon it. For example, we cannot exist without the sun's light and warmth. It is our duty, therefore, to think about nature and material creation seriously and to discover our relationship to them. If an individual fails to do this, we must suspect that he has too much self-doubt and fails to realise that he has enough time and energy to devote to the mineral, plant and animal worlds.

Since human beings are capable of misusing everything, we have the potential to exaggerate our devotion to nature. For example, a person can be so interested in animals that she forgets her fellow human beings. A possible explanation or rationalisation for this may be that she is disappointed with people.

With human beings
No human being becomes a human being in isolation from other human beings. We learn through, from and with others. The importance of our task of coexisting in harmony with others—in friendship, companionship and

120

in the wider society—should be well-known and accepted. Human beings, as social creatures, need to feel that they belong, and not only at work and in their marriages but in all the spheres of their life. For example, if a married couple have no friends in common, they end up experiencing not only increasing isolation but also a kind of inner poverty. The subject of understanding and relating to other people is dealt with in greater detail in my book on improving our social relationships.[42]

With oneself

'Man is, in reality, a spiritual being, and only when he lives in the spirit is he truly happy.'[43]

Nowadays even getting along with oneself is not something to be taken for granted but amounts to a real undertaking. No one has a natural gift in this area, and certainly there are few people these days who can say they live in peace with themselves. Somehow we are always in conflict, which manifests itself in an endless variety of symptoms, from unhappiness to insomnia, from nervousness to anxiety, from fatigue to tension, from social awkwardness to lack of willpower, from indecisiveness to guilt.

One of the main objectives of this book is to teach us how to live with ourselves better. Consequently this life task will not be discussed further here, since it is already a theme running through every page.

With the spiritual dimension, religion

'The inestimable value of religion is that when a man is vitally connected with it, through a real and living belief in it and in the Prophet who brought it, he receives a strength greater than his own which helps him to develop his good characteristics and overcome his bad ones. The whole purpose of religion is to change not only our

121

thoughts but our acts; when we believe in God and His Prophet and His teachings, we find we are growing, even though we perhaps thought ourselves incapable of growth and change!'[44]

What is the spiritual dimension? As we have seen in the discussion of the levels of existence in Chapter 2, the spirit is a part of the human being, an order in which human beings share and in which they can develop themselves. Spirituality rather than egotism should be our goal: the path from egotism to spirituality is called spiritualisation. It is difficult to encompass the spiritual dimension in words. To do so we need similes and symbols from a lower order, which can only provide the familiar lame comparisons. At the moment we still lack sufficient knowledge of the spiritual dimension, so that probably no one person could tell someone else just what it is. For this reason a number of examples are given to illustrate spirituality as it contrasts with egotism.

Egotism ⟶ Spiritualisation ⟶	Spirituality
I am right.	I consult with others.
I criticize others.	I love them.
I look at their faults.	I look at their positive qualities.
I judge them.	I distinguish the deed from the doer.
I get angry with others.	I try to help them.
I quarrel or give in.	I try to understand others.
I react.	I act as I myself decide.
I show my good deeds.	I conceal them.
I hide my bad deeds.	I admit them.
I see difficulties.	I regard them as welcome challenges.
I feel coerced.	I decide for myself.

122

I want to be free from something and thereby make myself dependent.	I strive for inner freedom.
I am the slave of my feelings, moods, emotions.	I am their master.
I become subjective.	I remain objective.
I focus on the past.	I live in the present.
I look for causes and reasons.	I look ahead.
I see no meaning in things.	Life and all that happens is meaningful.
I leave things to chance.	I arrange and plan.
I use my own private logic.	I use sound human reasoning.
I am a pessimist.	I am an optimist.
I hope.	I am certain.
I know what others ought to do.	I think about what I can do.
I have prejudices.	I look for the truth.
I only see the parts of something.	I see the whole, the entirety.
I pursue unconscious goals, e.g. the five immediate goals and the long term goals of my life pattern.	I determine my goals according to a sense of belonging, optimum personal development and the will of God.
My standard of behaviour is: superiority-inferiority	My standard of behaviour is: concern for others and fear of God.
I misuse my abilities.	I strive to fulfil my potential and serve others.
I am attached to the world.	I am detached.
I doubt.	I believe.

A. S. Eddington said in *The Nature of the Physical World*, 'It is difficult for the material physicist to accept the view that the basis of everything is of a spiritual nature. But . . . spirit is the first and most direct thing in our experience, and everything else is a remote conclusion.'[45] And Max Planck, decades ago at a convention in Florence, said:

Gentlemen, as a physicist, that is, as a man who has devoted his entire life to the most sober of sciences, the investigation of matter, I am surely free from the suspicion of being a religious fanatic. And so, after my research on the atom, I tell you this: there is no matter in itself! All matter only arises from and exists through a force which sets the atomic particles in vibration and holds them together like the tiniest solar system of atoms . . . therefore we must assume the existence of a conscious, intelligent spirit behind this force. This spirit is the very basis of all matter. It is not visible, transitory matter which is real, true, actual, but the invisible, immortal spirit! . . . I do not hesitate to give this secret creator the name that all peoples on the earth down the millennia have given it: God!

Of the place of the human race in creation it has been said that 'The human being stands on the highest level of matter and at the beginning of spirituality'.[46] The psychological techniques described in this book are intended to help readers achieve the goal of spirituality. They should be regarded as supplementary to the already familiar methods of service, love, understanding, prayer and meditation. To use religious terminology: 'By what means can man acquire these things? How shall he obtain these merciful gifts and powers? First, through the knowledge of God. Second, through the love of God. Third, through faith. Fourth, through philanthropic deeds. Fifth, through self-sacrifice.

Sixth, through severance from this world. Seventh, through sanctity and holiness.'[47]

What is religion? There are any number of definitions. 'Sect, church and denomination are sub-groups within one and the same religious sphere with a single founder, while different, independent religions are each characterised by having their own independent founder'. In other words we should not equate religion with the Church.

The English cultural historian Arnold Toynbee once described religion as a triumphal wagon which pursues a single, steady path upwards, while the various human cultures follow a cyclical path of birth, death, and rebirth. Kant put it this way. 'There is only one true religion, but there can be manifold ways of believing.' By 'religion', then, we do not mean the religious systems, denominations, churches and sects which the human race has developed out of the one religion, but that which the founder of a religion has taught personally as a prophet of God, that is, the eternal truth of, among others, Moses, Buddha, Christ, Muḥammad, the Báb and Bahá'u'lláh.

All religions teach us to do good, to be magnanimous, sincere, truthful, law-abiding and honest. So when we speak of 'the one religion' we mean that which is common to all religions as well as to each religion in its time and for a particular group of people.

A concern for religious issues has a place in the context of personal development because, as Goethe wrote, 'All epochs which are ruled by belief . . . are brilliant, heart-stirring and fruitful for their own and future generations. All epochs, on the other hand, in which unbelief claims a miserable victory disappear before posterity, because no one wants to be tormented with the recognition of the fruitless.' And Schiller stated, 'Everything totters when faith is lacking.'

Lack of faith is the greatest evil of our time. We lack faith

— in children, which discourages them and fosters egotism in them;
— in ourselves, which causes inferiority complexes, inhibitions, perfectionism and the wish to be right;
— in learning;
— in others, which results in aggression, fear of contact, depression and competition;
— in work, which is seen as an onerous obligation;
— in love and marriage;
— in nature;
— in the future and in the meaning of life, which leads to anxiety and pessimism, and
— in the spiritual dimension, in God.

Theodor Mommsen said, 'All the power as well as all the importance of democracy is founded on faith in ideals.' And Ludwig Börne wrote 'What is even the happiest person without faith? A beautiful flower in a glass of water, without roots and without duration.'

8

PRACTICAL EXAMPLES
AND CASES

Difficulties in speech and at work

A young man, terribly insecure, inhibited, and full of anxieties, was very dissatisfied with his job as a clerk. His chief symptom was a very bad stammer, especially in situations in which he did not feel he was in control. In such situations he opened his mouth and one waited in vain for something to come out. He was deeply discouraged as a child. He competed with a brother four years his senior and their mother's darling, whose practical abilities made him helpful around the house. His other brother, who was nine years older and his father's favourite, was the good son, successful socially as well as at school. This brother was regarded as a model of unattainable excellence. In short, his brothers held sway in the most important fields, being successful at home, in school and in social terms. Music was about the only sphere left to him, and he devoted his leisure time to pursuing music and the fine arts. His parents also contributed to his discouragement. His weak, compliant mother spoiled him as the baby of the family, and his father was extremely authoritarian.

His earliest memory was of feeling dreadful anxiety about finding his parents and of the helpful, comforting grandfather who led him to them. His second memory was of being with his mother at the doctor's, of whom he was terrified. His third memory was of being alone and 'having to' go to sleep. He rebelled against this, but only passively, in that he got up and walked around without anyone noticing.

His flying dreams revealed his ambition and his falling dreams his feeling of not belonging. He dreamt of being pursued and being unable to run. How difficult life was and how little he could do! Not even run away! Naturally embarrassment dreams also belonged to his 'repertoire', signifying his fear of making a fool of himself.

His life pattern revealed the following aspects: I'm just a little boy and not particularly well equipped by nature. I can't imagine ever becoming a real man. Life is difficult and I must rely on other people's help. And yet I have to be careful, because the world is evil and unjust and does not always have good intentions towards me . . .

Five weeks after he had begun to understand his life pattern and practise the personal development techniques, his speech improved so much that his impediment hardly ever showed. He only experienced difficulties with it if he had to telephone a particular superior. He coped with this problem by making an effort to get to know this man better on a personal level. He was thus able to ascertain that his superior was pursuing immediate goal 3 (establishing superiority), by coming across as especially sure of himself and thereby covering up his own inner insecurity.

Some weeks later, to his astonishment, the young clerk realised that he was actually quite happy with his work, having developed a much more positive attitude towards it. After that he no longer thought about changing jobs.

Fear of illness

A very nervous young girl suffered from irrational fears, especially the fear of illness and death. As the middle one of three children she grew up competing with her domineering older sister. The middle child was ambitious and achievement-oriented and distinguished herself at school both academically and athletically, while her sister had more friends, among whom she was the leader. In this way the sisters had divided the world outside the family between them, so that the role of the dear, sweet, obedient child in the family fell to their younger brother. The middle sister dominated her brother, who subordinated himself to her, but in any event she soon realised that she was 'only' a girl and developed the so-called 'masculine protest', that is, she feared having to play an inferior role as a girl. Consequently she had practically no friends.

Her earliest childhood memory was of lying happily in her bed and seeing a branch of the cherry tree in front of her window laden with shiny red cherries. She realised that the tree did not belong to her and that she could not pick cherries from it. No one was present. The next three memories were all fearful ones. In one memory she was sitting behind her sister on a merry-go-round horse. The sister was able to hold the bridle, but she had to hold on to her sister. She slid farther and farther backwards and cried from fear until her father jumped on to the moving roundabout and took her off. In another memory she was afraid of blood poisoning, and was being helped by her mother and the doctor. The last memory she had was of being afraid of her aunt, because she had lost a bracelet the aunt had given her as a gift.

The last three memories clearly show her fear of life and other people, and her low self-confidence. She too needed help from others and was unable to do very much by

129

herself. This was even evident in the apparently positive first memory. Was it not unjust that she was unable to pick any cherries?

After four weeks of practising all the personal development techniques she felt so much better that the periods of despondency which had previously crippled her became the exception rather than the rule. Her dreams became more positive. In the following three months she became worse only two or three times, in the worst case for three days. After about six months she felt satisfied with the world and with herself and was convinced that she was finished with any relapses. Fear of illness and death no longer played any part in her life.

Professional and marital difficulties

A young, very despondent man was no longer getting on with a friend who was also his business partner. In addition he was worried that he was drifting farther and farther apart from his wife. After only about two weeks of practising personal development, most of his problems appeared to be alleviated. He had realised that they stemmed from his own negative attitude. His wife was considerably more positive, so their married life quickly improved when he too began to cultivate a positive outlook.

His professional life improved as well, once he realised that he had felt inferior to his friend. His self-confidence increased and he made himself more independent of his friend and his friend's opinions, so that the entire relationship between them normalised. He became calmer and less moody, no longer worried so much about the future, felt more love for his wife and, to his own astonishment, had more time for himself.

The tendency to dominate

A woman was dissatisfied with herself because she was always catching herself finding fault with her husband and giving him orders concerning his work. Because of this he became discouraged and his work deteriorated further, so that she began to despise him. The quality of their life together deteriorated more and more.

She acknowledged that it was not her responsibility to order her husband about in this manner, and she decided to work on herself instead. Soon she realised that she was a perfectionist and learned to leave well enough alone, especially when she saw how her behaviour and love of order were making her husband increasingly passive and untidy.

After a few months of therapy the atmosphere in the house changed completely. She managed to refrain from grumbling and dominating. Her husband became more responsible in his work once he no longer had to contend with her criticism. Even under the pressure of work they had more to say to each other and were increasingly devoted to one another, something that had previously happened only on holidays.

Anger

A young man tended to become angry very quickly and suffered as a result from stomach pains. He was afraid of doing something wrong and being laughed at, and tended to blush in the company of others. He also wanted to change his occupation but did not dare speak to his parents about it.

His earliest memories were of quarrels between adults during which he felt helpless. He also remembered being attacked by a dog and needing medical help. He was once badly treated by a playmate (to whom he otherwise felt superior) in the presence of an older boy, and was laughed at by both of them. Finally he remembered being attacked by a swarm of wasps and getting stung more than his playmate who had trampled on the wasps' nest. His life pattern included the following aspects: I'm just a little boy and must rely on other people's help. I need people's recognition and must therefore be good. Life is dangerous and difficult. Even other people can be threatening and unjust, so I must be very careful.

After six weeks of practice, especially with the first and second techniques of personal development, he became angry much less often and his general condition improved. His occupational preferences were taken into account and a short time later he was able to begin training in the profession of his choice.

The 'masculine protest'

An attractive young working girl who lived alone suffered from 'circulatory disorders' and nervousness. She had developed many symptoms, including anxiety, insomnia, fatigue, insecurity, indecisiveness, a short-temper, the inability to concentrate on driving, or to think clearly, and the feeling that everything was too much for her to cope with. Her physical symptoms included cold hands and feet, nausea, diarrhoea and stomach pains. She had lost ten kilos in four months.

She had two older sisters with whom she competed. The oldest was both good at home and successful in school. The middle one realised that her chance to succeed lay in the social sphere. She was the leader among many girl friends, and was charming, athletic and popular. There was nothing left for the youngest but to be a tomboy. So as a child she was awkward, recalcitrant, wild and rebellious, always playing boys' games and coming home with her clothes torn. Her sisters had married long ago, but she had persistent bad luck with her boyfriends and always broke off with them after a short relationship. Her dreams were often of a sexual nature and included aspects of hindrance dreams as well.

She had early childhood memories of her entire family being shocked by her behaviour, of being punished in nursery school because she was cheeky to a boy, of getting a thrashing from her father because she had waded barefoot in puddles, and so on.

After about eight weeks of therapy she had become reasonably familiar with her life pattern and things began to look up. She no longer used her circulatory disorders as an excuse, her cold feet improved and she slept well. She behaved with self-assurance, no longer became so tired while driving, could finish projects, and developed more initiative. Previously tense relationships with her parents, friends and acquaintances were resolved through discussion. She felt more balanced, became more cheerful and even gained weight back. As to her greatest problem—relations with the opposite sex—she became generally better prepared to take sensible steps to find a partner.

Inhibitions

Ever since his divorce a young man had been suffering from depression and a fear of choking and was extremely inhibited about making decisions. After the divorce he went back to live with his ex-wife because he was unable to decide on a separate flat. Moreover, he was completely lacking in any kind of drive and, to his own amazement, was not even interested in women any more. To make matters worse, he had a constant fear of swallowing the wrong way as well as terrible inhibitions about speaking in front of people he was connected with at work.

Through his earliest memories he became familiar with certain aspects of his life pattern and achieved good results in only two weeks. He freed himself of his dependence on his ex-wife and found his own flat. His fear of choking improved through the use of the first technique of personal development. Encouraged by his initial successes his attitude to life grew more confident and he began to see that it was really not that important always to be certain. He soon became more comfortable making decisions. With the help of the second technique he realised that he had been using his inhibitions to attract attention. His inhibitions subsided almost immediately he became aware of this previously unconscious goal.

Lack of respect in marriage

An attractive young woman was unhappy and in a state of nervous tension because her husband was indifferent to her and spent all his free time drinking with his friends. No matter what she did, she got no recognition from him at all. Her self-confidence was shattered and she cried a good deal.

Soon after she began to work on herself she made the decision to become independent. She found a good job and soon afterwards, her own small flat. She felt considerably happier and more relaxed. Suddenly something happened which puzzled her at first: her husband began to pay attention to her and became much more positive towards her. He gave up his excessive drinking and wanted to move in with her. She was basically in favour of this idea, but decided to leave him on tenterhooks for a few months so she could be sure their mutual goodwill was not merely temporary.

Inhibitions in speaking

A young man experienced difficulties speaking in front of his equals or his superiors. At such times his throat felt constricted and he felt generally anxious and tense, but managed to finish what he had to say nonetheless. Helped by the three techniques, he soon recognised that he had developed an excessive desire for security. He acquired a feeling of superiority in a devious way by telling himself—unconsciously of course—that in spite of his fear of speaking he still succeeded in looking good in front of others.

Disappointment

A young girl experienced crushing disappointment when her boyfriend of long standing left her for another girl whom he married after a brief courtship. The rejected girl went through such a crisis that she withdrew completely. For a while she was not even able to work.

With the help of a counsellor she was able to see how she herself had contributed to the situation of her boyfriend leaving her. In reality she was unwilling to get married because she was afraid of having to assume a subordinate role in the marriage. She never quite got over this fear, but she did become satisfied with herself and with life in general, got up in the mornings with no difficulty and made contact with many old and new acquaintances of both sexes.

Marital problems

A married woman was experiencing difficulties in her marriage, which was hardly functioning sexually at all. She wanted to be loving to her husband but found herself unable to manage it. She felt pressured whenever she was with him. She was depressed and exhausted, and was finding it difficult to get to sleep. She had no time for anything besides housework and consequently had hardly any contact with other people. She had a more positive attitude towards her husband than she had towards herself.

She began to use the personal development techniques and, on the basis of what she learned about herself, was able to initiate a discussion with her husband. This was so productive that every aspect of her marriage improved almost immediately. Her difficulty in falling asleep disappeared when she no longer needed exhaustion as an excuse to avoid sex. She began to enjoy housework and got through it more quickly and efficiently. She felt much happier in general and she and her husband began to cultivate contacts outside their small family circle. Needless to say, her husband contributed to this rapid transformation through his positive attitude towards his wife.

The stupidity reflex

A young man, an only child with good educational achievements, considered himself to be stupid and incompetent and consequently had problems at work. He was unable to concentrate, had no interests, began to stutter and often felt depressed.

After about three months of therapy his job went better, and his depression and self-pity disappeared. Above all he no longer thought himself stupid. His success was primarily due to the fact that he gathered up his courage and found an inoffensive way to persuade his indulgent and domineering mother to stop treating him like a child.

Nervousness

An extremely nervous young woman was very dissatisfied with her marriage. She was no longer able to see anything positive about her husband, only his faults.

It took her about three and a half months to change her attitude. Without being conscious of this change her husband reacted positively, becoming more considerate and more attentive to her, and their mutual love was soon re-established. They were able to discuss their problems, and even ran a business together, and the wife's relationship with her in-laws improved noticeably. Her weight loss, which had previously been a cause for some anxiety, stopped and she gradually regained her normal weight. Today both she and her husband face the future with optimism.

POSTSCRIPT

The previous cases have been described in a simplified form in order to help the reader understand and practise the personal development techniques recommended here. It has already been emphasised that human beings can misuse anything, and this includes personal development. It should only be used as a means to the ends of finding better ways to live together, of increasing both our personal courage and our concern for others, of developing our consciousness and spirituality, and of strengthening our faith. This book should not be used as a substitute for medical or psychotherapeutic treatment. Moreover, it would be an abuse of the principles of personal development to become so preoccupied with self as to forget one's life tasks and responsibilities. Increased egotism would be the only result of that. If we gave in to such self-centredness, life would pass us by; we would live neither in the past nor in the future, but we would have no present either. When Buddha lay dying his disciples asked for his last words, as a sort of final testament. Among other things, he is believed to have said, 'Do not look into the past, for it oppresses you. Do not look into the future, for you cannot recognise it. Look at the present, and see how beautiful it is.'

NOTES

1. Erik Blumenthal, *To Understand and Be Understood*, Oneworld Publications, England, 1987.
2. 'Abdu'l-Bahá, quoted in *The Advent of Divine Justice*, by Shoghi Effendi, p.32. US Bahá'í Publishing Trust, 1971.
3. 'Abdu'l-Bahá, *The Promulgation of Universal Peace*, p.184. US Bahá'í Publishing Trust, 1982.
4. Ibid., p. 293.
5. Jean Gebser, *The Ever-present Origin*, USA, Bastard, Noel & Mickunas, 1985.
6. Shoghi Effendi, *Citadel of the Faith*, p.130. US Bahá'í Publishing Trust, 1970.
7. See note 5 above.
8. Bahá'u'lláh, *Tablets of Bahá'u'lláh*, p.138. Bahá'í World Centre, Israel, 1978.
9. Bahá'u'lláh, *Gleanings from the Writings of Bahá'u'lláh*, p.143. UK Bahá'í Publishing Trust, 1978.
10. 'Abdu'l-Bahá, quoted in *The Divine Art of Living*, p.48. US Bahá'í Publishing Trust, 1960.
11. R. Dreikurs and Erik Blumenthal, *Eltern und Kinder—Freunde oder Feinde?* Ernst-Klett Verlag, West Germany.
12. Bahá'u'lláh, *Gleanings*, p.148.
13. Ibid., p.29.
14. 'Abdu'l-Bahá, *Paris Talks*, p.176. UK Bahá'í Publishing Trust, 1969.
15. Ibid., p.129.
16. Bahá'u'lláh, *Gleanings*, p.259.
17. Erik Blumenthal, 'The Significance of Age Difference in Twins', Institute for Applied Psychology, Zürich, Switzerland.

18. The Báb, quoted in *The Dawnbreakers*, p.65. UK Bahá'í Publishing Trust, 1953.
19. 'Abdu'l-Bahá, quoted in *Bahá'u'lláh and the New Era*, by J. E. Esslemont, p.80. UK Bahá'í Publishing Trust, 1974.
20. Bahá'u'lláh, *The Hidden Words*, p.52. Oneworld Publications, England, 1986.
21. See note 1 above.
22. 'Abdu'l-Bahá, *Paris Talks*, p.35.
23. Ibid., p. 16.
24. 'Abdu'l-Bahá, *Star of the West*, Vol. XI, p.18.
25. Bahá'u'lláh, *Gleanings*, p.325.
26. Ibid., p.94.
27. 'Abdu'l-Bahá, *The Promulgation of Universal Peace*, p.168.
28. Shoghi Effendi, quoted in *Lights of Guidance*, p.388. Bahá'í Publishing Trust of India, 1983.
29. Shoghi Effendi, quoted in *Living the Life*, p.14. UK Bahá'í Publishing Trust, 1974.
30. Bahá'u'lláh, *Gleanings*, p.276.
31. Ibid., p.81.
32. Adapted from the work of R. Dreikurs.
33. 'Abdu'l-Bahá, quoted in *Bahá'u'lláh and the New Era*, p.77.
34. Bahá'u'lláh, *The Hidden Words*, p.52.
35. See Chapter 4 of *To Understand and Be Understood*, (note 1 above) for a more detailed discussion of this subject.
36. R. Dreikurs, *The Challenge of Parenthood*, Hawthorn, USA, 1979.
37. Bahá'u'lláh, *The Hidden Words*, p.107.
38. R. Dreikurs, *The Challenge of Marriage*, Hawthorn, USA, 1978.
39. Bahá'u'lláh, *The Seven Valleys & The Four Valleys*, p.58. US Bahá'í Publishing Trust, 1975.
40. 'Abdu'l-Bahá, quoted in *Bahá'u'lláh and the New Era*, p.154.
41. Bahá'u'lláh, *Tablets of Bahá'u'lláh*, p.142.
42. See note 1 above.
43. 'Abdu'l-Bahá, *Paris Talks*, p.72.
44. Shoghi Effendi, quoted in *Lights of Guidance*, p.419.
45. A. S. Eddington, *The Nature of the Physical World*, Darby Books, USA, 1981.
46. 'Abdu'l-Bahá, *Some Answered Questions*, p.235. US Bahá'í Publishing Trust, 1981.
47. 'Abdu'l-Bahá, *The Promulgation of Universal Peace*, p.226.

ACHIEVING PEACE BY THE YEAR 2000
John Huddleston

If mankind were to decide to establish peace in the world by the year 2000, what practical steps must be taken now – by individuals, politicians, governments and international agencies – in order to achieve that goal? What options would be open, and how could the concerned citizen contribute to this important process of change?

These are the questions addressed in this highly topical book. John Huddleston, Chief of the Budget and Planning Division of the IMF, presents a penetrating analysis of the causes of war and the role of the superpowers in contemporary politics and puts forward a twelve point plan for establishing world peace.

Of special interest to all those active in the peace movement and the campaign for disarmament, this thought-provoking and timely blueprint for peace is essential reading for anyone concerned about the future of mankind.

ISBN 1–85168–006–3   paperback   128pp   £3.50   US$5.95

TO UNDERSTAND AND BE UNDERSTOOD
A Practical Guide to Successful Relationships
Erik Blumenthal

To Understand and Be Understood presents a refreshingly original approach to social life today. Written by an internationally respected psychotherapist in a warm, anecdotal fashion, this book offers down-to-earth, workable advice for successful, loving relationships.

The author brings the reader a new understanding of himself and others based on simple, easy-to-use principles, illustrated throughout with real life examples drawn from years of professional practice. A valuable handbook for all those seeking more aware, understanding relationships in all spheres of their lives.

Erik Blumenthal, a practising psychotherapist, lectures at the Alfred Adler Institute in Zurich, and is currently President of the Swiss Society for Individual Psychology. He is the author of a number of books on child-rearing, self-education, marriage and old age.

ISBN 1–85168–004–7   paperback   160pp   £4.50   US$7.50

SCIENCE AND RELIGION
Towards the Restoration of an Ancient Harmony
Anjam Khursheed

Over the last two decades, exciting discoveries in modern physics have challenged scientists to reconsider some of their most basic assumptions about the nature of the universe – and of man. It is in the light of these recent developments that Anjam Khursheed, himself a research physicist at the European Centre for Nuclear Research (CERN) in Geneva, reviews the traditional conflict between science and religion in Western society.

Science and Religion is a fascinating and well researched account of that conflict, focusing on man's present predicament and escalating global problems. Of interest to both the scientist and the general reader.

ISBN 1–85168–005–5   144pp   paperback   £4.50   US$7.50

THE HIDDEN WORDS OF BAHÁ'U'LLÁH
Bahá'u'lláh

This exquisite collection of meditational verse is perhaps the best known work of the founder of the Bahá'í Faith, written in 1858 whilst exiled to Iraq from his native Iran. For years only a few hand-written manuscripts survived. Now, however, it has been translated into sixty-nine languages, with over 100,000 copies sold worldwide.

Designed by the award-winning Nicholas Thirkell, and selected as one of the best designed books in the world at the international exhibition of books in Germany in 1987, this is the first de luxe gift edition of a remarkable work which offers wisdom to guide every seeker through the constant struggle of the spiritual journey.

ISBN 1–85168–001–2   112pp   Cloth   £8.95   US$13.95

THE PROMISE OF WORLD PEACE
The Universal House of Justice

This beautifully produced, sumptuously illustrated book is an unusual mixture of fact, photographs and a plea for peace. In a world beset with escalating global problems it offers a verbal and visual presentation of the need for positive action.

The text, originally written and privately circulated by the governing body of the Bahá'í Faith, represents an analysis of humanity's current predicament and an outline of the attitudes and decisions which need to be adopted to secure world peace. Acclaimed by heads of state, politicians, royalty, religious leaders and philosophers worldwide, its noble and radical appeal to the better nature of humankind has been rendered into forty-five languages.

ISBN 1–85168–002–0   192pp   120 illns   paperback
£6.95   US$10.95

DRAWINGS, VERSE & BELIEF
Bernard Leach

Here we have a testament to a life spent discovering 'the unfamiliar groundwork of humanity in search of truth and beauty'. Born in Hong Kong in 1887, Bernard Leach was a potter of world renown whose life and work bridged the traditions of East and West.

Leach's sensitive illustrations and verse reflect a richly varied life travelling and living in both continents. The illustrations in this volume cover a period of sixty-three years, capturing in delicate pen and wash scenes of rugged English landscapes and lazy summer days, tranquil Japanese lakes, snow-capped peaks and busy harbours. The earliest poem dates back to 1907, penned by a young man of twenty, while the later verse reflects a man of mature years, sight failing, dwelling on the meaning of life.

This beautiful, cloth-bound gift edition combines the author-artist's delicate visual images and delightful verse with an impassioned profession of faith, to provide a rare insight into the personality of a great master craftsman.

ISBN 1–85168–012–8   160pp   82 illns   Cloth
£12.95   US$19.95

ONEWORLD PUBLICATIONS

Oneworld Publications publishes contemporary books on cultural, philosophical and social issues. We focus on peace and global concerns, personal development, the family, spiritual awareness, religious questions and the Bahá'í Faith. For further information about Oneworld Publications books, please write to the Mailing List Dept at Oneworld Publications, 1c Standbrook House, Old Bond Street, London W1X 3TD, England.

Some Oneworld titles you may enjoy:

Science and Religion Anjam Khursheed	US$7.50	£4.50	☐
To Understand and Be Understood Erik Blumenthal	US$7.50	£4.50	☐
The Way to Inner Freedom Erik Blumenthal	US$7.50	£4.50	☐
The Hidden Words Bahá'u'lláh	US$13.95	£8.95	☐
The Promise of World Peace The Universal House of Justice	US$10.95	£6.95	☐
Achieving Peace by the Year 2000 John Huddleston	US$5.95	£3.50	☐
Drawings, Verse & Belief Bernard Leach	US$19.95	£12.95	☐
The Secret of the Stolen Mandolin Barbara Larkin (Children's fiction)	US$3.75	£2.25	☐

All these books are available at your local bookshop or library, or can be ordered direct from the publisher. Just tick the titles you want and fill in the form below:

Name (Block letters) _____

Address _____

_____

Send to Oneworld Publications, Cash Sales Department, 1c Standbrook House, Old Bond Street, London W1X 3TD, England.
Please enclose cheque or bank draft to the value of the cover price plus postage & packing:
UK: 15% for orders up to £20 and 10% for orders over £20. Maximum postage £5.
OVERSEAS: 15% on all orders.
All payments should be made in US Dollars or Pounds Sterling.